Hope & Possibility
Through Trauma

By Don Shetterly

BTS Publishing
(**B**reaking **T**he **S**ilence)
Deltona, FL.

To contact the publisher:

BTS Publishing
c/o Don Shetterly
PO Box 5176
Deltona, FL. 32728

BTS@donshetterly.com

http://www.donshetterly.com

Acknowledgements

This page is dedicated to all those that have been there with me through each step of my journey. There are so many individuals that if I began to name a few of them, I would undoubtedly leave out some along the way. Some of the people that were there for me in these times were people whose names I hardly knew, but their contributions were beyond comprehension.

There are, however, some individuals that need to be mentioned as my life would not be all that it is without our paths crossing. Some individuals come your way for a brief moment, and some are there traveling beside you from moments that were beyond the stars.

People such as Dr. Paul Canali who I not only consider as a healer in my life but as a very close friend and mentor. By him sharing his life with me in the way that he has, I have learned that there are truly good people in the world. He has shown me that there are pure forms of love for another human, and has modeled it through his own life. Through his healing work, my life has been given hope and possibility that I did not realize existed up until that point. I celebrate all that life has to offer as I offer my thanks to him for just being human – an evolving human!

Then, there is my partner of many years, who has stood by me and loved me with the purest and truest form of love. He's been my confidant, my companion and has helped me grow in so many ways that I could never have imagined. He has been an enormous help and resource in putting this book together, and has given selflessly of his time in reviewing and editing my words. I will be forever grateful in my heart for his life touching my own.

Many thanks also go to Chelsey Rockwell-Román for giving of her time to help finalize the beautiful book cover.

Table Of Contents

Chapter One: Introduction

Chapter Two: Hope Of Possibility

Chapter Three: Self Acceptance

Chapter Four: Rewiring The Brain

Chapter Five: Personal Growth

Chapter Six: Our Body Connections

Chapter Seven: In The Moment

Chapter Eight: Connections

Chapter Nine: Music Connects Us

Chapter Ten: Listening

Chapter Eleven: Abundance

Chapter Twelve: Special Moments

Chapter Thirteen: Closing Thoughts

Chapter Fourteen: Resources

Chapter Fifteen: Discussion Guide

Index

About The Author

Into The Journey
Of
Hope And Possibility

You Travel Not Alone

By Don Shetterly

You travel not alone.
They are there to guide you.
You notice how it feels,
You sense how it is,
You travel not alone.

No matter the time or day,
Not a moment goes by,
When you don't realize –
You're held in arms of love,
Connected from on high.

The birds and trees know it,
The ocean feels it,
The sky stretches with awe,
As you connect from your heart
You travel not alone.

Chapter One

Introduction

We all start from a tiny fragment of substance, and find ourselves created into a work that is ever changing and evolving.

<u>Selected Writings</u>

What This Book Is About

Who Is Dr. Canali

My Story

What This Book Is About

Over time, my life has evolved through some traumatic experiences. With each moment, I have used writing to help me deal with these situations and find my way through them. Often the road was not as clear and visible as some of these words depict. Many of these writings came after I had come through some of my most difficult moments.

In this book, you will not find a step by step account of the traumatic moments I lived through from an early age, even though you'll get a glimpse into my story at the beginning. Instead, you will find writings that came out of these various moments of my healing, and what led me to further realizations that there could be hope and possibility through trauma. When you view the selected writings as a whole, you will see a picture form that shows traumatic experiences in our life do not have to be an end point. In fact, they are often a launching point to a greater awareness and opportunity we have in our life, if we allow them to be.

When I sat down and wrote these various writings, I never thought that I would publish them in a book. Some of them were published in the newsletter of the former Voices In Action Organization. As I shared my words, I found that I enjoyed doing this, and I also learned more about myself along the way. In the early days, I was so afraid of sharing these.

Many of these writings may have appeared on various blogs, and things that I shared online including the "Mind Body Thoughts" blog that I write for daily. They were part of my daily journey that I shared openly with others. It was about reclaiming my personal power in life and discovering more fully who I was.

Some of my more recent writings are coming from my morning meditation time. I always take a clipboard with a blank piece of paper on it, and even though I have nothing specific on my mind to write about, I find that words often flow from my hands. I find that the words are often what I need to hear for that day. They are a communication that I open myself up to and allow.

The idea for this book came together through a series of events that were not connected. It is not a book filled with scientific facts and research. This book is about life and the struggles we face. It is also about the healing, hope, and possibilities that exist within us. I'm sharing the words in these selected writings with the world, and hoping that they touch someone's life in a way that changes their current moment -- giving them hope, possibility, and the choice for a new moment for their lives.

Who Is Dr. Canali

One of the people you will see me reference throughout this book is Dr. Paul Canali, of Evolutionary Healing Institute in Miami, Florida. Anyone that knows me will probably have heard of Dr. Canali. He is an individual that has helped me change my life in so many ways that it is difficult not to share him with the world.

While I have high words of endearment for Dr. Canali, I realize that it is I who has found my way through the healing and awareness that I have. It has been my journey of discovery and growth in some of the most difficult and darkest of moments. However, Dr. Canali is a very safe person who is so accepting, and has been there with me in many of those difficult moments.

What makes the work he does, Unified Therapy™, so life changing is that Dr. Canali has learned how to help people connect with their own master healing system that resides within each person. In many ways, he is a guide holding the space open so the person can go in and experience all that they need to, in order to bring about healing in their lives. He is able to walk through the depths of the fire with you, as you attempt to find the footing on your own path. Of course, the work he does is much more than this, but it is very difficult to put into words.

When I began seeing Dr. Canali in 2004, my life was a mess. Emotionally, I struggled to hold it together, and cursed the fact that I was a very sensitive person. I had migraine headaches constantly and had suffered from headaches since I was a child. Road rage and anger were some of my close companions, which I tried to hide from those around me. Depression and anxiety attacked me with a vengeance, making it so difficult to be around people and in crowds. I suffered from allergies that required regular medication just to breathe at times. My shoulder had so much pain in it that some days it was all I could do to raise my arm very high. Back pain was a constant in my life, as well as hip pain and neck pain. Tense muscles were just as common to me as breathing was. Relaxation was something I longed for, but had no idea how to achieve.

On top of that, touch was as difficult to me as just about anything I suffered. I could feel very little touch, and that which

I did feel, was very scary to me. It took me a long time to begin to fully feel touch in the way that I do today. Without the work of Dr. Canali, I would have never realized just what was possible in the area of physical touch, with healing bodywork, or found between two people.

I could go on forever about how this work has changed my life but there would not be enough pages to write everything. What Dr. Canali gave to me and helped me with has now become the focus of my own healing bodywork, as a licensed massage therapist. It has also helped me discover myself as a music artist, writer, and overall highly creative person.

My life is still evolving and growing in ways that I would never have imagined many years ago. I never thought any of this was possible. The more I discover about myself, the more I see, realize, and become consciously aware of. There is so much more out there than many humans realize. We are all meant to be much more than we currently are. We are all meant to evolve, grow, and shine from the highest mountains.

My Story (To Be Continued)

It all started on a warm, sunny, late summer day. The horrendous events leading up to this time would forever change my life! These events were not just what had happened in the previous couple of months, but also things that had happened a long time ago in my life. However, the more recent events played such a key role in what would happen this day.

Sitting through the church service was excruciating; not for what the preacher said, but because my back hurt with extreme pain. It was more pain than anyone could ever imagine. I sat there during the church service just hoping that it would go away. A couple of Tylenol, which normally stopped the pain, did not have one ounce of effect on me that day.

So when I finally got home after avoiding so many of my friends, giving an excuse of having so many things to get done, I left church and went home to take a nap. I was so tired.

Little did I realize, this nap would be a life-changing point, after which no day would be the same as before. For once I shut my eyes, a new world was rotated into view: a world that was nothing I had ever known or experienced before.

Upon waking up from my restful nap, I felt somewhat refreshed. Even as this feeling felt good, I realized that I had wasted so much time that day. There was too much to do and accomplish for me to be taking a nap that afternoon. As I sprang to my feet, something unexpectedly terrible happened! The pain was gone from my back, but surprisingly, so was the strength in my legs.

Lying on the floor in a very stunned state of mind, I pulled myself back up to the couch. Not being one to give up, I once again sprang to my feet, although just a little slower this time, thinking that I had not completely awakened. Once again, THUD! I dropped to the floor!

Stunned and shocked, once again I tried to stand up, and once again I hit the floor! As much as I fought the idea, I knew there was something wrong. I knew that there was no way my feet and legs would hold me up. No matter what I did, I could not stand up!

The days and weeks after that turned into an eternity of darkness and hopelessness for me. Doctor after doctor, and test after test, kept coming up short of answers on why all of this was happening to me. Some thought it was Multiple Sclerosis and others had absolutely no clue what was causing this condition. After a ride in the ambulance, due to seizures and much shaking and trembling taking place in my body, the hospital released me to come back home. They claimed there was nothing wrong with me. MRI's were done and again, nothing was showing any conclusive results.

It was not just my feet now that would no longer hold me up. My arms did not have the strength or energy to do much. It was a struggle just to stay awake, as each moment I felt very tired. Soon, my speech and thoughts were becoming slow or nonexistent.

Finally, a neurologist admitted me to the hospital for observation and to run more tests. Going to the hospital was like a breath of fresh air because up until this point, all the doctors were doing was sending me home to my apartment. The only thing wrong with that is I could not take care of myself. I found it humiliating to have people that were family and friends taking care of me in some very personal situations.

Upon entering the hospital, the doctors began more tests. At one point, I could not even answer a simple question the doctors asked, "What is your name?" I could not even feel them sticking a pin in the bottom of my feet to test my sensitivity or reflexes.

Regardless of the tests that the doctors did, no one came up with answers. I still could not walk, stand, or even talk in a normal manner. Physical therapy was started but it seemed to do very little for me.

Nothing seemed to work until the neurologist, Dr. Elaine Wilson, asked if I had been through a lot in my life. By that time, I knew deep down that there was a connection to what I had been through and the paralysis. It was just very difficult to admit this. The neurologist asked if I would like to talk to someone, and I managed to get out the word "yes."

Soon a psychiatrist by the name of Dr. Bradley Diner, showed up in my room to talk. I still cannot remember what we talked about that day, but what I do recall is that on this very same day, I began to take my first step in physical therapy. Up until this point, I had not been accomplishing much in physical therapy. To me, it was no coincidence. In my mind, beginning to talk to Dr. Bradley Diner and taking the first step were strongly connected.

At age 26, I lied in the hospital, wondering if this is all my life would hold for me from now until I grew old enough to die. Would I just lie here in the hospital like a vegetable, not being able to take care of myself? I had so many goals in life that I had not accomplished, but now it seemed as if they would never see the light of day. Life appeared hopeless and a struggle that I wasn't sure would ever improve.

The psychiatrist came to visit me each morning to talk. I realized that there were many things I needed to talk about but I was so frightened to say anything. I feared what my parents might find out, and I had already learned in life that you did not talk to others about family problems. In many ways, I did not want to face any of these horrors!

However, I knew that it was time either to choose talking about these things, or to choose my own death. My brain was already shutting everything down in my body, and death was not far off. I remember thinking to myself that I had a choice to make. The choice was somehow to find a way through this, or to give up and let myself remain in the form

I was in. Of course I knew deep down that if I did not make a choice, that the choice would be made for me.

One final muscle strength test the doctors were performing was excruciatingly painful for me. The lady that was performing the test seemed to treat me only as a test subject and not as a human. Because it was so difficult to talk, I struggled to get any words out. This made it very difficult to get her to stop her tests on me, as they were overwhelming to me. As she kept the test up, my body did the only thing it knew how to do, and that was to escape. When I woke up, the doctors were saying "clear", and I saw the paddles coming down toward my chest as they were getting ready to shock me back to life. My brain struggled to understand what had happened, but one of the nurses told me that they thought they had lost me. I knew I had not gone anywhere, because the entire time, I was in a bright light watching all that was going on.

From that point forward, life had a different meaning to me and I knew that I had to make it through the paralysis. I had no idea if I could fully recover from where I was at, but I had hope and optimism that I would fully heal. I knew I had to plunge into the darkness to find myself and to find freedom. Of course, this could only happen one step at a time.

Through a stay at the Bridgeway Psychiatric Hospital in Little Rock, Arkansas, and therapy, I started to deal with the ugly pieces of life that I had been running from all my life. It was not an easy process, and to explain the full process of healing would take an entire book.

I am a survivor of child sexual abuse. It began when I was around five years old, and was home because I was fighting the chicken pox. My father was taking care of me while my mom was working. When I woke up that day, I was lying in a pool of blood, as my father was trying to clean me up and get rid of the evidence of what happened. Later, we would go to the house of a friend that my mom worked with, a Registered Nurse, for antibiotic shots, because I was becoming very ill. There was no way my parents wanted to take me to a doctor for fear of the questions that may get asked. It was during this time, that I was held back in school from first grade to kindergarten because I could not do first grade math.

When I was around 7 or 8 years old, I was forced to stand in the bedroom of my parents while they had sex. To this day, I am still as horrified at the image of this as I was then. At the time, I thought my father was once again hurting my mom, and while I wanted to run and hide, I was not allowed to leave the room.

Around age 13, I remember being raped again by my father. This became the nightmare that I faced for many years before I finally found a way past it. At first the nightmare dealt with me being afraid of the color purple, which was the color of the bedspread that my face was shoved into while I was being raped. It took me many years to get strong enough to confront this nightmare.

It was at this time that my older brother began showing me how to masturbate, and what that meant. At night, he would somehow coax me into his room and get me to do this on myself or on him. I still don't remember how he was so crafty at getting me into his room, because I had to walk past my younger brother and my parents' bedroom doors to get to his room. No doors were allowed to be closed in our house, so how anyone didn't know this was going on, is still beyond my comprehension. Maybe my family did know it was going on and chose to stay silent.

These nighttime sessions would go on almost every day, or if not every day, they were frequent. If my older brother and I were alone or driving to church, he would often pull off onto a side gravel road and these episodes would continue. He showed me how to perform oral sex, and would expect me to do this on him. I still remember the sight and smell of his body, which nauseates me to this day. No matter how badly I wanted to get away from this, there was no one to talk to because we were taught that you did not talk about these things.

My father enjoyed talking about masturbation with me when I was a teenager, and would constantly question me about it when we were alone. I still remember the time, when I was riding in his semi truck on the way to Montana, and he pulled off to the side of the road and demonstrated masturbation on himself to me. I was a captive wanting to run, but not being able to go anywhere. After all, we were in the middle of nowhere and not only was it late at night, but there was not a person in sight for many miles.

There is so much that I went through, and these are just some of the bigger moments that I can recall. My father was a very angry and abusive person that would often hit me for just about anything that I did or didn't do. I was beaten with belts, and his fist, and hit with a garden hoe or boards, or whatever he could get his hand on. Verbally, he constantly berated me and put me down through his constant criticizing.

I still remember the time when I was very young, and he took my older brother out to a shed on the acreage we were living in, to punish him. Even though the shed was some distance from the house and the windows were closed, I could still hear the screams of my brother. They still haunt me today. It was a sound that no one ever wants to hear.

In addition to how he treated us, my pets lived in fear of my father. They knew that if they got close to him, they would experience the angry side of him, or worse, they might face death.

Those little kittens that my father killed one night when I was very young will forever remain in my mind. I was busy washing dishes, as he and my mom went outside to the cellar that night to get something, or so they said. It was while they were outside that I heard their whispers of making sure all the kittens were accounted for, as they allowed the heavy cellar door to slam on them and kill them.

My precious kittens that I loved and that loved me were killed as I washed the dishes. Hearing their screams, I tried to hold back the tears, fearing what would be done to me if I was caught crying. My parents came back in the house and acted as if somehow all the kittens were in the wrong place, and the door slammed on them and killed them. I was supposed to go on and live like nothing had taken place but deep down, I knew what had happened. Their screams would haunt me for years to come.

There were many moments in my life that I blocked out, and most likely I still do block them out. Dealing with horror and trauma in this way is beyond comprehension. It is an overload on my mind, and that is what caused the paralysis (also known as a somatoform disorder or conversion disorder). My mind kept trying to hide all that had gone on from me. In this abbreviated story, I've only shared some of what happened. There is so much more.

As a result, it took me many years of intense healing and counseling to begin coming through these things. I lived in fear all my life that if I spoke about these things, someone would come after me. I still deal with the fear, but I am coming to a point in my life where I will not be silenced any longer. If my abusers do not like me sharing this, it is their problem. I can no longer hold these things in.

Through the times that I was trying to come to terms with all that happened, my family pulled every trick in the book to bring me back in line. They threatened me and shunned me. I was given the silent treatment. They tried to make me feel ashamed that I somehow was accusing them of being terrible people. In reality, my father and older brother had an evil side to them, but when you are raised to be dependent upon the family, breaking free from this shame and guilt is very difficult.

At one point, the toxic letters were arriving so frequently that I would have anxiety attacks just going to the mailbox. I was already suffering from deep depression, and just trying to fight my way back into my life. Every day was difficult and I did not need the crap that they were writing to me in letters. It was at that point that I cut off all communication with them. It was one of the hardest things I ever had to do, but I knew that in order for me to survive, I had no choice.

In the past few years, I have made tremendous progress in reclaiming all that I am. It began with going to massage school and continued through the trauma recovery work that Dr. Canali does. Slowly but surely, I began to reclaim those parts of my body that had been so traumatized. As I have done this, I am finding a sense of freedom, full of hope and possibility, unlike anything I have ever known. At one time, I was not sure if I could heal from these wounds and scars on my life, but now, I see there is a way through.

Today if you saw me, you would never be able to tell that I was confined to a wheelchair and almost died. You would see someone that has forged through so many things, has survived some of the worst events imaginable in life, and is living proof, there is a light at the end of the tunnel!

Yes, I still get tired and stressed from all these things. Sometimes the pains and traumatic moments I have suffered through in life still get difficult. But I know that the only way out of the darkness is to take one step at a time. I know going into the fear is the way through it. I know that you can stand me up at the gates of Hell, but there is no way I'm going to back down.

Many people ask me what keeps me going or why I don't give up. These events are what keep me going, for all I have to do is take a look back to those days of paralysis and realize if I could come back from that point in my life, I can do anything.

I realize that I now have a second chance in life. What I make of my life now is up to me, and solely up to me! I can choose to run from things, or I can embrace them! I can choose to continue down paths that I don't want to follow, or I can turn around and take a different path. I can choose to fight healing in my life, or I can seek the help that I know I need.

None of this is easy! But I know I must go on because I am not ready to die, and I have no desire to sit in a wheelchair again with everyone taking care of my every physical need! I know I must go on! I must put one foot in front of the other and take one step at a time, even though it may be the hardest thing I do!

My story does continue to unfold in ways that I could never have imagined. The tremendous growth, awareness, and healing that I am now experiencing has changed my life dramatically. No longer do I allow the fears of life to control it, and no longer do I hide within my cave. My life has become one of intense growth, which not only translates to me personally, but to all that I meet. It is a story that is ever changing, and one that I will not even come close to predicting how it will appear tomorrow. For each day that I am alive, I am comforted to know that I can evolve and grow if I allow myself to do this. *(Written on 9/3/10)*

Chapter Two

Hope Of Possibility

----

*We've seen ordinary people do extra-
ordinary things and accomplish tasks
that were nothing short of impossible at
the time.*

<u>Selected Writings</u>

The Hope Of Possibility

Through Deep Layers

Can I Make It?

Rocket Blast

Do We Change Or Hunker Down?

The Will To Survive

Concerns And Worry

A Process, Not An End Point

In Difficult Times We Blossom

Not A Life Sentence

Our Life's Storybook

The Hope Of Possibility

Have you ever looked at your day and your life, and said "that's not possible, there's no way I can ever do that?" If you haven't, I would be surprised as I think this is a pretty common thing for most humans to face at some point or another in their lives.

Yet, throughout the history of the world, we've seen ordinary people do extraordinary things and accomplish tasks that were nothing short of impossible at the time. There are so many examples of this.

So, if we view something as impossible, how do we go from impossible to possible?

We might conclude that one would need to believe that what we want to do is possible, and that having the right mindset is the key to beginning the journey. However, I know there have been many times in my life that I could not see the possibility of something, to get myself started. In those times, I relied on hope that there was a hope of possibility to get where I was going, and that's about all I could muster up the strength to do. Even in these moments, this was almost too difficult to do.

So what if we took a moment to acknowledge something in our life that we view as impossible today, and maybe hold for just a moment that there is a hope that it may be possible? Just holding that thought in our mind gives us a different energy and potential than viewing something as impossible. Whether what lies before us can be accomplished, we will only find out as we travel the journey that lies before us.

We don't have to know all the answers in that moment, or be able to see things with vivid clarity. All we have to do is offer ourselves that the hope of possibility exists, and allow our journey to unfold before us. That's it! That's all! Yes, we may have our doubts and we may have our pains, inflictions, and boulders standing in our way, but those don't concern us at this moment. The only thing we need to stay focused on is that the hope of possibility exists within us. The rest will find its way.

So my challenge to you today is to not just accept what I'm saying as gospel truth, but to test it within yourself. See if this works or if it doesn't. Test it. Try it and challenge it. Find that part within your mind that says "this is not possible," and then replace it with "I have hope that it is possible." Let the rest unfold as it will on its own, and in its own time. There is no need to control or manipulate the events, but to just allow them to happen.

I celebrate the hope of possibility to each person that reads this. *(Written on 1/15/10)*

Through Deep Layers

Have you ever looked at something through a microscope? I remember during science classes in high school and college, looking at all kinds of things from little bacteria to many types of objects. Through the naked eye, we were able to see something much different than through the microscope. Even with the various power adjustments of the microscope, we could see many layers of whatever it was we were looking at. More powerful microscopes allowed us to look even deeper into an object.

Just like looking deep into an object through a microscope, the same could be said that this is exactly what healing is all about. It is going through the layers and then when you think you've seen everything, adjusting the power and going deeper yet. As you go deeper, you see things that you were not even aware of, or realize existed. Yet, they are there.

So go deeper than you have gone so far! See what all there is to see in your life and find that which you do not know exists. Then see just how far down the rabbit hole you can go. *(Written on 7/01/10)*

Can I Make It?

A week ago, I was wondering in life if I would ever come to a point in my healing where things really changed in a way where I could go "that's it - I've got it!" I was beginning to get frustrated and tired of this process after several years of working intensely on things. The entire ordeal of the rash that started a few months back was almost the last straw that I could take.

Life was not easy for me, and these recent developments have pushed my limits to the max and made me question everything that I know as well as all that I have learned. I am a person with great courage and determination to go through all that life has given me, but some of these recent events challenged me to the point of near exhaustion. There is a part of me that understands the higher purpose for this, but when your body becomes weary and bruised to the bone, the capacity to go on is diminished.

So many people in my situation or other situations often give up or turn to alcohol, drugs, work, or other things to numb themselves. I had my own ways that I numbed myself out. It may appear that it is far easier to just numb one's self than to find the strength and courage to face these things head on. However, if we continue to run from the fear and numb our pain, then we are only inviting a life full of heartache, despair, and one that just seems to be too much to deal with.

Trauma changes our biology and it alters who we truly are as a person. Child abuse and trauma take the power away from the victim, rendering them as participants in their body but not in control of who they are. No matter what that individual desires, without going into the process of fully discovering, acknowledging, and releasing all that has gone on, these things will continue to hold power over the individual. It is like a short circuit in the brain. The effects of trauma are biological, physical and mental.

But just as I was coming to the end of my rope, the question of another blog entry, Are You Ready To Let Go? (See page 47) came front and center with me. A war was waging that day within me, during my session with Dr. Canali, to let go of something that I could not put into words. However, I knew it was there. At the same time, it was difficult even to begin thinking about letting go of it. After all, it was something I had known for many years, and it was something that was such a part of me.

So as the session continued, I found myself being very sensitive to all that was going on, but still feeling like I was coming up against the short circuited part of my brain; the part that said, "You'll never get through this - you can't do this - you're not worthy - you just won't make it - you're not good enough!" As badly as I wanted to let go of that part of me, I realized just how difficult it was, because it had grown so interconnected within me that to pluck it out meant I had to give up something that was so attached. As the session went on, Dr. Canali did acupuncture on me and my body was so afraid of it, that it was hunched over trying to protect itself. My body was literally shielding itself from the acupuncture.

When I left the office that day, I felt discouraged because I didn't really think we had made any progress. By the time I got home from the five hour drive that night, my neck, shoulders, arm, and back were in pain. They were stiff and sore, and I began to blame it on sitting in the car for that long.

Of course by the next morning, the anger was coming through in full force. I felt like I was pissed off the moment I woke up, and really didn't understand why. My body ached and I felt horrible. Of course, Dr. Canali reminded me that this was all part of the process and not to go into the fear of it. He encouraged me to work on myself on the table, which I did, and that helped a lot. He said by the next day I would feel much better, and I did.

I woke up that next day feeling much lighter, freer and completely different than the day before. In the past, I've had moments where I felt better and more free and more relaxed, but somehow, I knew this was different. It was a feeling of being connected to my heart and just not overwhelmed like I normally am. I noticed the anger was not anywhere near the level I normally have to deal with. It was a strange feeling and unusual, because I don't think I have ever experienced it before.

Several days later and through a very stressful week, I'm still feeling very light, connected, and centered. It is hard to explain but it is a wonderful feeling. This is a week later and it is still with me. I'm noticing that I'm able to talk to people and not feel so shy or nervous, or sense the complete terror in my stomach. I'm noticing that I'm seeing people in a different light than I ever have, and that feeling is coming from compassion instead of judgment and fear.

Anger has been replaced by a willingness to be in the moment, not be bashed around by the moment. The source of anger seems to be dwindling and decreasing unlike any other moment in my life. I've had experiences in the past few days where I've had some deep connections with people I hardly know, and felt confident enough to share things that I do understand.

I'm experiencing a confidence in myself unlike any I've ever witnessed before. The stress of the week did not cripple me. In fact, the stress just seemed to flow through and out of me. Yes, I felt the emotions at times and the effects of it but it didn't stay. It didn't last. If I acknowledged it, I noticed that it just sort of went poof!

As I shared this with Dr. Canali today, he reminded me that what I'm experiencing is normal and it is the way life was intended to be. I'm thinking - wow - I like this! Bring this on some more! Give me more of it!

Once again, to bring this point home in a crystal clear way - - this is not something that I get my mind to focus on, or wish for, or do whatever else that many other people do.

It is something that has come from the inside out at the core level of my being. It is not something I'm doing or creating - it is just happening and it is just coming from the true part of who I am. It's almost boggling to my mind to think about, let alone experience.

I'm sure there will be some more bumps along the way and I may stub my toe on the rocks in the path but for now, this is one heck of an experience. To think a week ago, I was at the end of my rope, and to see where I am now is making me want to jump up and down for joy! Sometimes we truly need to get to the end of our rope in order to find out there's a ledge to stand on below us. It takes a lot of courage and faith to let go of the rope, but if we don't we'd just tire ourselves out, all the while missing the ledge to stand on below.

And the best part about this is all of this is real! It isn't someone's idea of what it should be or some result of some method that gives you warm fuzzies. It is a part of the core of my being. It is now a part that shows the real person I am. It comes from deep within and now it is part of me. I am reclaiming my life and for the first time, I'm truly getting a glimpse of what that life is about. It's beautiful and it's a joy-filled moment that is deeply rooted within me. That's the part that makes it so special, because when our experiences and our healing are deeply rooted within the body, they are as real as you can get! *(Written on 2/25/10)*

Rocket Blast

Take a look back in your life to something that was a struggle for you to get through. The more difficult it was to get through, the better example it will be for this exercise. Now, look back and see just all the rough spots, the difficult moments, and those times when you didn't think you could go on. Just focus on that for a moment.

Now bring yourself to this very moment where you are at in your life and see just how far you've come. How did you get from that point to where you at this moment? Maybe you went through some intense anger, or maybe you struggled with what to do for a long time and then you just said, "that's enough, I'm going to do steps x, y and z." Maybe you weren't even sure what steps y and z were at that moment. And maybe you weren't even sure what step x was, but you knew you needed to do something.

So what happened here? First of all, you got in touch with the emotions that you were feeling. Whether it was the anger or determination or whatever it was, you felt that. Feeling the emotion of where you are at is a very important step. It gives us the energy, the courage, the faith to take the next step. Without it, we'd be like a car running on an empty fuel tank. And when new direction is needed in your life, sometimes we need a rocket blast to get us moving forward. Sometimes low gear just won't get us there. *(Written on 7/20/10)*

Do We Change Or Hunker Down?

Many of us from the species called humans come up against big obstacles in our lives and in our days. We all know what these things are, if we have not become completely numb to them. I'm sure each one of us could think of a zillion obstacles, or at least one, in our life right at this moment.

These obstacles are put in our path for many reasons. Sometimes they are there to get us to stop and look at the direction we are traveling. Other times, they are put there so hopefully we will gain something new from observing the obstacle. They might, as well, be put there for many other reasons, from bringing new insight to us, a warning for our lives, or just to get our attention. I'm sure each of us could come up with many reasons for these obstacles being put in our path.

We as humans are meant to evolve and grow and become more than we were the day before. In the busy hustle of life, evolving and growth toward things higher than ourselves often get put on the back burner. There are just too many things we tell ourselves that we must do, and stopping to look at the obstacles in our life just requires too much time, work, and energy. Okay, it may not be that directly that we do this, but I'm not telling anyone something new. We all are well aware of what we do, even if we don't own up to it.

So my question is reflective for each person who is reading this. Do we change or do we hunker down? Hunkering down can be a good thing, sometimes, when the hurricane force winds are bearing down upon us, but if we stay hunkered down, we'll never see the sunlight of the new day. Once again, I ask, do we change or do we hunker down?

It is up to each one of us not to be content with the status quo in our lives, and not to just accept our life as the means to an end, or the way it has been and always will be. It is up to each one of us to go forward in our lives, reaching for that higher purpose within ourselves, and becoming all that we are not only meant to be but that we are capable of becoming. There is so much that lies within each one of us and we often forget this. We all must realize just how much we do have, in spite of the obstacles we see before us.

So one final time I ask the question again: Do we change or do we hunker down when we come upon obstacles in our lives?

It is an answer only you can give, and hopefully you are honest with yourself because no one else will do that for you. *(Written on 11/22/09)*

The Will To Survive

There are many people in this world that have been through extraordinary circumstances, and in some cases it's almost too difficult to believe that one can endure as much as they have. Yet, even in the midst of many things that people have had to struggle against, most find a way to make it through what they have encountered.

I'm sure most of them would say that the trying times were difficult beyond belief, and at the time they didn't feel as if they could make it. However, in some way, in some manner or fashion, these people made it. They survived. They had the will to survive.

Today, I'm probably writing this for myself as much as for anyone. My life is no stranger to adversity and situations that an average person could not fathom, let alone experience. Some people cannot even begin comprehending some of the things that I have been through and to be honest, my mind sometimes has much difficulty understanding all of it as well.

I think back to my early days on this planet, when I was subjected to all kinds of conditions that a child should not have to endure. During those times, I learned how to numb out, to escape and not be present. It was my way of surviving events that were just too difficult for anyone, let alone a child.

Then I'm taken to the point where I became paralyzed, and realizing that from one day to the next, we just never know what can happen. I found out then that life can change in a dramatic way, giving us challenges which we were not prepared to face. And through those moments, the strength and courage come to help lift us slowly from this time and place. It is not without its trials, tribulations, and weariness that one has to find the will to survive.

I'm reminded of the times that the will to survive included the need not to commit suicide. Even though I tried many times, I was never successful and it was in those worst of moments that somehow, something inside of me kept me going. While many may credit it to a religious figure or what not, I learned that whatever it was that kept me going was deep within me. It was that faintest of faint moments where my life said, "no - it is not your time - you must keep going." It was in those moments where the will to survive met the horrible evil secrets my life was holding. That meeting of two opposites, created the spark that ignited enough sustenance to continue.

Even now as I continue my own healing and I go deeper into the process, I find that time and time again, I come up against some of the worst moments of evil I have fought so hard to forget. I could continue to try and play hide and seek with them, but I know that sooner or later they will find me out. It would seem to be the easier way to deal with them, and may feel like it, but in the end, it comes down to how far I'm willing to allow myself to travel through my own journey. And believe me, there are many days when I say, "this is too much - this is more than any person should have to deal with."

Sometimes I have no clue where the will to survive comes from, or how I even find the spark to ignite it. Sometimes, it seems as if there is absolutely no hope, no way forward, or no idea to begin the way forward into hope. Sometimes, all that seems to appear is a void of blackness with a lifetime sentence of futility.

It is in these times when I realize that I may need to crawl back into my bunker, and plot the next course of action. It is in these times, when maybe all I can do is look down at my feet and see they are still planted on the path of my life's journey. It is in these times, that just making it through the day is accomplishing as much as building the world's tallest mountain range.

I've even witnessed the will to survive in many animals I cared for, on farms that I managed. If the animals still had the fight left in them, and I mean the fight of wanting to stand up or just drink water and eat some food, then they had a chance. The animals that did not have this fight, seldom made it. The fight was half the battle, and the rest of the battle was their body healing and mending itself.

So if you're facing the dark, doom-filled glare of the void of darkness in your own life, know that this too shall pass and that you can make it through this. Allow yourself to stop and crawl back into your bunker while you plot the next course of action. Or if that is too much to do, allow yourself to look down and see that your feet are firmly planted on the ground below you. Give yourself the moment to be there without any expectations of what to do next. Give yourself the option to do this.

I'm not here to tell you that all of life will be easy, or these difficult moments will be a piece of cake. I'm not here to tell you to pull yourself up by your bootstraps or chin up, because I know it is much more difficult than that. Most likely it is a difficult time and the despair is knocking on your door. However, just know that this too shall pass and you can make it through it. Remember, the fight is half the battle and as long as you kick, scream, yell, and push or whatever it is that you do - you will find your way through it.

And if you think you can't find your way through it and there seems to be no open doors, just closed ones - then look for a window! *(Written on 2/10/10)*

Concern And Worry

Are you worried and concerned about things in your life? If you're like I am, and probably many others, why not try this exercise?

Find a quiet place, and make a list of all the things that concern you, or you are worried about. Nothing is too great or too small to list. It doesn't have to be a complete thought or sentence. It could be just words, pictures, or however you choose to record it. Allow yourself time to list everything you are concerned about. It is easy to worry about the things in life we are concerned about, but sometimes we forget we can release these as well.

Here's a thought to consider after you have listed your concerns.

What if I released my concerns today to the angels and just let these things go? For I know that the more I worry about these things, the more it robs me of precious energy. I cannot control them. If I let them control me, then I have allowed myself to become their slave. What if I released my concerns today to the angels and just let these things go? Trust them. Trust the angels.

And if the word "angels" does not translate for you, try inserting the word that works for you. It may be "the universe", "God", your higher power, or some other phrase. It does not matter what the word is specifically as much as the thought and action behind this. *(Written on 7/12/10)*

A Process, Not An End Point

At one time, I thought that if I just worked on particular issue A, B, and C, that I would be fully healed from baggage of my past. It seemed as if all I had to do was go to counseling, work on it, become aware of it and that's it. I would be healed. While I would love to believe this, along with millions of other folks on this earth, healing really doesn't work this way.

For you see, once you begin to work on things, then you stand before a new world that opens up and unfolds itself. Imagine never being able to see, and then all of the sudden you get your eyesight. Everything that before was unknown to you is now vivid before your eyes. Imagine how that might look. You're still standing in the same world you have always known, but now your awareness of what is around you has unfolded many times over.

Healing works much the same way. As we begin to take back those areas of our lives that were damaged or stretched out of proportion, life begins to look differently. We discover new things about all that is around us, as well as ourselves. We begin to become more aware of all that there is instead of all that we currently know.

With each new awareness, and each new level of awareness, there also come other parts of our past issues that may not yet be resolved. It does not mean we have not fully healed, or that we just need to move on. It means that we are growing, changing, and coming up on opportunities to take our lives further. Growing, changing, and evolving make us more human, and even though they may offer some rough moments in life, the rewards are full of possibility.

So often, we feel that we just want to move beyond things and not feel all of what may be coming up. Sometimes we may need to do this momentarily to survive, but if we continue this way, we are only robbing ourselves of all that can be. Sure, it isn't always easy, but we can heal and we can grow if we allow it. In all reality, the more we keep ourselves from feeling the uncomfortable stuff in our lives, the more we feed energy to these things.

Often, I have had people wonder why I continue to go into all that life has given to me, and continue bringing these healing moments out. Part of it is my determination to move beyond these things, because I am intimately aware of how they affect all aspects of my life. The other part is that I know there is a higher purpose to all that I've gone through, and I am guided by this.

While I cannot fully see the higher purpose for myself, deep down the prompts in life show me that it does exist and to keep going. It does not make any of this easy, nor do I enjoy spending the hard hours working on this. In the end, though, I know that I can either rest on my laurels or I can dive head first into the evil side of life that was thrust upon me --- and reclaim awareness greater than I can currently comprehend.

I remember the words to the song that Garth Brooks sings, "The Dance": "I could have missed the pain but I'd of had to miss the dance." It is a beautiful concept, because while there are rough moments in our lives, it is a dance. The more we allow the bad and the good into our awareness, the more we can grow, prosper, and claim all that is ours. There is so much more in life than we are currently and often noticing. However, all too often we just see the pain of it and we try to flee from it. It is when we stop and embrace the pain that we fully "dance" in life.

As I said in the beginning of this, healing is not an end point. It is a process. If you are experiencing the pains in your life and the connections to past events, then most likely you are being given the opportunity to grow and discover yourself in new ways. Yes, I realize it may be scary and difficult, but give it all you have and discover the rewards that await. Life does try to get our attention in one way or another and if we ignore it, we will see that it just tries harder. May you listen to life as it tries to get your attention, so that you become all you can be as a human, and continue to evolve and grow in awareness. To do so, makes you truly human. *(Written on 3/08/10)*

In Difficult Times We Blossom

This past winter was a tough one where I live, and many of the plants took a big hit. We had been down in the low to mid twenties (Fahrenheit) for many days, which is unusual for us. While most places get much colder than that during the winter months, our vegetation is not designed to survive these colder temperatures. By the time spring had come, so many of our plants were brown, leafless, and appeared to be dead.

At first glance, one would have thought they were all dead and needed to be replaced. After all, there was very little left to each plant. There was no sign of life. It looked grim for them. My thoughts began to turn toward digging up what was left and replacing the plants.

Then the strangest thing happened. As the temperatures warmed up and the spring rains fell, I began to notice some life in each plant. This did not happen all at once, but began to show up little by little. With special care and extra water, many of the plants continue to grow again, with some doing better than others.

Isn't life the same way? We go through moments where our feet are walking in the fire. We think there is no tomorrow and no hope for improvement. Yet, the strangest thing happens - we blossom! Somehow through all the rough moments when it appeared we could not make it, we noticed some new life. We noticed new growth. It just showed up without any fanfare or announcement.

Just as the plants know how to send up new shoots of growth or fill their branches with leaves, so too do our human bodies and minds. We are complex, biological organisms that have far more power to heal, grow, and recover from some of the worst situations imaginable.

Consider those darkest and most difficult times in life that you may have traveled. I'm sure that while you were in the midst of those moments, it appeared there was no way through. Yet, during these times, many parts of your life were growing and preparing you to blossom.

It is a beautiful thing about humans that we have the capacity to take some very rough moments and turn them into beauty. We are much stronger, more resilient and full of courage than we often realize. Everything we need is within us, located in our mind, our body, and our spirit. May we cherish, honor, and love all that we are and all the growth we have experienced. *(Written on 7/01/10)*

Not A Life Sentence

It is part of our journey, not a life sentence!

How many times do we go through life struggling and feeling like we're never going to get "there"? Of course, I'm not sure if I have figured out and understood where "there" is at, but we all try to aim toward it. Sometimes "there" seems to be like a moving target. When we are in the midst of the struggle, it seems like there is no end.

Yet, I'm reminded again (I think this makes like reminder one million and some) that all the difficulties and struggles I face are just part of my journey. As long as I don't stop for good on my journey, I will get through them. It is okay to pause and rest awhile, but as I know, we must keep moving along our journey.

Even when we feel like there is not one single person that is there for us, or wants to be around us, and we feel so all alone, we can take solace in knowing that this is not a life sentence, but it just part of the journey.

I'm not saying it will be easy or quick, or magically it will get better at the push of a button, but things do improve. Sometimes you have to walk through the valley of the shadow of death to get to the beauty that lies beyond it. Sometimes you have to walk through this without people that fully understand what the valley looks like.

In all things, though, realize just like I do that this is part of the journey, not a life sentence. *(Written on 1/30/10)*

Our Life's Storybook

Many years ago I was seeing a therapist by the name of Emma Wallace, RN, MS. She told me a wonderful thought in regards to some difficult moments I was experiencing. At the time, it seemed like I had made some bad choices and thought that there was no tomorrow. How many times has each one of us felt like we had really messed up our lives?

I remember her telling me that each day we get to write in the storybook of our lives. If what we write today is not something that we are happy with, then each day we are free to write a new chapter. We can include whatever stories or situations we want, as well as any colors that we wish to put in there, for tomorrow's chapter has not yet been written. We write it with each day that passes. Tomorrow is a blank page. It is waiting for us and it does not matter what we wrote the previous days. It only matters what we write on the blank pages that we are given.

Life is a series of events, choices, reactions, and growth. While one event can impact our future, it does not mean that it will control our future. Our days are what we make them and how we view them. It is up to us to choose how we live our days and what we bring into our lives. Yes, there are periods of mourning and difficult times, but if we choose to keep moving forward, we are still writing the chapters in our storybook of our life. And with each day that passes, we get to keep coloring the pages in a different and unique way that is all up to our thoughts, our moments, and our hopes.

For me, the choices that I thought had messed up my life turned into a major turning point. I could not see it at that early moment, but as I look back now, if it wouldn't have been for those choices, I would not be experiencing the life I am today. There is hope and possibility out there! *(Written on 7/20/10)*

Chapter Three

Self Acceptance

----

*One of the noblest acts of kindness we
can do for the world is to learn how to
completely love and accept ourselves.*

Selected Writings

Prayer Of Self Acceptance

Limitations Upon Ourselves

The Beginning Of Our Path

Perspective On The Healing Journey

Confronted With Something New

Garage Sale

Are You Ready To Let Go?

Throw The Garbage Out The Window

Putting A Puzzle Together

Prayer Of Self Acceptance

Dear Angels,

It is a difficult time right now and I could use all the support and love I can get at this time. Between the physical pain and the everyday stress, I feel like the weight of the world is upon me. I feel as if the hope of tomorrow is waning. I feel battered and bruised.

Yet, I am thankful for so much in my life. There is so much good that I have and which is around me. I appreciate all of it.

Please help me to accept myself and help me to see myself as you see me. Please help me to not just notice my faults, but see all of the good I have in myself. I realize there are many fears that I hold on to, but help me find the courage to let them go.

Wrap your arms of love around me and show me once more, just how special I am. Surround me with the courage to face my fears and the hope to see it through. Help me to open myself up and accept all of it in.

Thank you for listening and hearing me. *(Written on 7/13/10)*

Limitations Upon Ourselves

How many times do we sit there and wish we could do something about our situation, only to draw the conclusion that there are a hundred zillion reasons why this cannot happen? Have you ever done this? I'm sure if you are like most other humans, you probably have at some point in your life. Yet, do we even notice that we do this, or has it just become commonplace for us?

When we were born, we were given all the tools we needed to do whatever it is that our lives were meant to do. With time and through the influence of our caregivers, we began to doubt many of these abilities. As we carried on in life, we began to let these limitations build up on one another, preventing us from living our full potential in life.

Many times we go through our day, not even aware that we are placing these limits on ourselves. It can be through self talk, or even the activities that we allow ourselves to participate in. It could be in the choices we make that keep us extremely busy from morning to night, so that we inadvertently limit our choices of what we really want to do. Sometimes these things that limit us are beyond our visible comprehension, and even if someone points it out to us, we do not have the frame of reference to understand fully that which we cannot see.

My challenge to each person reading this, and to myself, is that we begin to become acquainted with all the limitations we put on ourselves. Once we become aware of them, then it is up to us to choose to let these limitations go and embrace something greater within ourselves. *(Written on 12/15/09)*

Perspective On The Healing Journey

One of the things that was extremely difficult for me when I was in the thick of my healing, was seeing that something was actually happening and that I was moving forward. Often when we are in the middle of a major change in our lives, we cannot always see what is going on. It is not until after the major change has taken place that we are able to look back and see exactly what took place. Having a way to help gauge what is going on in our life helps to bring us a sense of hope, because we can more readily see the progress.

Imagine for a moment if you were going to start out on a trip of walking from the Atlantic Ocean to the Pacific Ocean, tomorrow. Would you expect yourself to be there by tomorrow or the next day or even the next week? Would you be able to completely plan and identify all that you may or may not encounter? Would you be able to name all of the roads and cities you may or may not travel down? The answers probably seem obvious, but they are very important because if you apply the same questions to your journey of healing, it will help give you perspective about what is going on in your life. You would probably understand that it takes many days to get from the Atlantic to the Pacific. Along the way you might want to sit down and take a rest, or you might take a turn that puts you in a direction you didn't intend to go. You probably would encounter unknown storms and objects as you traveled on your journey, as well.

I remember during my counseling sessions, my therapist, Emma Wallace, was always throwing out ideas for me to help myself during the times I was not in therapy. Most of the ideas were like, "yes that sounds good," but I never took most of them and used them. Then one day, she brought up an idea which just grabbed a hold of me. I remember getting out of the counseling session and heading straight to the store to buy the supplies I needed. When I got home that night, I began the project.

You do not need to be an artist of any kind, just someone who knows how to use a colored marker. I'm not an artist by any means, and the point isn't to make a beautiful piece of artwork, but to make a useful piece of navigation for your life.

Go out and get yourself a big sheet of paper at the store. Make sure you have a big enough wall to put the poster on when you are finished. If you don't have some nice big color markers, crayons, or colored pencils, make sure you get some of those as well. Put on some nice music that you like to listen to and allows your thoughts to flow freely, as it allows your mind to relax. Get yourself comfortable, and make sure you have plenty of time without distractions to do this.

You are now going to divide your paper into three sections. You can be creative in how you do this, and if you feel like you messed up, just buy another sheet of paper and do it again. Remember you are not an artist striving for perfection. You are just trying to make a useful piece of navigation.

On the left side of the page, you will want to designate it as something along the lines of "your current land or where you are currently at". Be creative and label it to match whatever you feel it should be called. Then on the right hand side, label it something along the lines of "dreamland or where you want to be". In the middle of the paper, draw yourself a nice long and wide walking trail. You can make the trail curve around, or just design it however you want it to be. Allow yourself to be as creative as you can be, and just be in the moment. Don't forget to sign and date your paper in some area, showing that this is completely your own possession and it belongs to no one but you.

Once you have the framework completed, go back to whichever side of the paper that might be the easiest for you to start. Again there is no hard and fast rule to this, but just follow your intuition and instinct.

On the current situation, draw, write, or paste pictures describing where and how you currently see yourself. Draw or place objects in here that describe things that make you up as a person, and define who you are at this time. These can be positive or negative, and when you are done, it will give you a good representation of how you currently see yourself. Make sure you leave some space open so that you can add to it as time goes.

In the dreamland section, begin drawing objects that depict where you want your life to be. These would include things that you wished were true in your life, or you hope you will get to through healing. They don't necessarily have to be things that you know you can obtain, but things you desire, or things you would love to have as a part of your life. Make sure you do leave open space in this section, because as time goes you will most likely want to add to it.

Once you have these sections completed, begin the middle section (with the long, walking trail) by placing little pictures of feet, or even rocks in here. You don't have to place much in here at this time, as this will be something you will continue to fill in as time goes. Whatever you feel is an appropriate representation of your project and your life is what you would use here. These things will be the obstacles, or the fears, or whatever it is that you have to encounter as you go from the journey of your current land to your dreamland. As you figure out what these things are, you would give the feet or the rocks or the object a name of what it was, and put a date that you found it as well.

When you are finished, hang this up in a location that you will pass by many times each day. It should be secure enough on the wall that you can add to it, as well, just by getting one of your colored markers or pencils. Make sure you keep your colored pencils and markers very handy and close by.

As you go through your days, weeks, and months, and as you identify more objects to place on the poster, just take a moment and fill them in. In time, you will begin to see just how valuable this is, and when you get discouraged about the progress you are making, all you have to do is take a look at all the steps you have taken or the rocks you have uncovered.

This is a very simple representation of your healing, and it helped me so much in keeping myself going during the times I was ready to give up. When I could take a look at the poster and see just what had been going on, I would have renewed hope that I was getting somewhere, and before long the poster told a very detailed story of my healing journey. *(Written on 5/08/04)*

Confronted With Something New

We often see things around us through our own eyes, and the filters of life that we have experienced. Who can blame us, though? These are our tools, our paint brushes, and our frames of reference to view everything as a comprehensible piece of information. Without these things, we would miss out on that which we see, because it would not compute in our minds and through our eyes.

The challenge we face as humans, though, is to understand that which we cannot truly see, and that which is not clear to us. Whether it is a new concept we have not learned, a spark of an idea that does not have defining edges, or someone else going through difficult times, each of these things is an opportunity for us to learn, to grow, and to really understand who we are as individuals and how we fit in with the things that are fuzzy.

When we are confronted with something new, let us see if we can define the edges of it so that we have a better understanding of what it is that we are looking at. Let us not be afraid, but welcome the newness with an open mind, an analytical heart, and the curiosity of a child.   *(Written on 10/11/09)*

Garage Sale

I am offering the following for sale. Name your price and you can have it! Actually, if you want any of these things, I might even give them away free!

1) My shortcomings as a human being, when I forget my place in the universe, or how I use or abuse the resources around me in the universe.

2) My fears that I carry around all the time as extra baggage, though I get so tired of carrying the heavy load. I'd actually pay someone if they could just help lift these darn things off my back for a day!

3) My insecurities about my life, my friends, my intimate relationships, where I feel everyone is going to abandon me, leave me, tell me to leave, or just not want to be around me.

4) My thinking that everyone, if they are not talking to me, is talking about me to others or behind my back or in whatever ways they can. This is definitely a family heirloom, so it should sell for a considerable amount of money.

5) My anger, mood swings at times, and over frustration with the little things in life.

6) My extreme sensitivity when I can't stay grounded, and when everything around me hurts or feels harsh, or it seems like unknown entities are out to get me. This includes the sensitivity of seeing things around me hurting.

7) My lack of confidence in talking to people in real life, feeling like I don't know enough, can't form the words to say, or just feeling afraid of what they might think, how they might react, and what they might or might not think and say. This also includes those times when the words just won't form in my brain, and my hand seems unwilling to write them or my mouth unwilling to speak them.

8) My feeling of still trying to find my way in the world, and some days feeling like it is all coming together, with other days feeling like I'm lost in a cloud of confusion. I will include the cloud of confusion for free.

9) The ability to be close and intimate with others without being afraid of what they might or might not do, and being afraid I may get physically and emotionally hurt.

10) Will include the fears of a million different things too numerous to list. Inquire within to browse these items.

I decided to write this because it seems like I carry these things around constantly, and while I say I want to give them up, for some reason I cling to them. And yet, I know that if I acknowledge these things as present in my life, I then have the option to work on releasing them. While I would love it to be an immediate process, where I would be completely free of these things, I know it is a step by step undertaking which I am doing.

And I remind myself of just how far I have come in releasing these things. *(Written on 6/22/08)*

Are You Ready To Let Go?

To read more about the rash and itching that I experienced, please see my blog posts on January 5, 2010 at mindbodythoughts.blogspot.com, "Body Memories, Abuse Memories and Trauma Recovery". This particular account was written after I had been struggling with a rash and itching that would not go away.

The other day, I went in for a session with Dr. Canali and I proudly displayed what was left of the rash I've been dealing with. He looked at me and said, "Are you ready to let go of that today?" At first, the question struck me as odd and my immediate response was of course "yes, I am!"

However, as I sat there and thought about this like I do with everything, I wondered in my mind if I was really ready to let go of it. It was hard being honest with myself because deep down, I wasn't sure if I was. Here I had responded to Dr. Canali that I was ready to let go, but part of me said – "you really don't believe that, do you?"

Once I got on the table, I looked at Dr. Canali and stated that "you know I thought I was ready to let go of it but to be completely honest, I'm not sure if I am." As I explained, this rash seems like a part of me, just like any other body part. To let go or get rid of the rash means I'm giving up something about myself, and if I do that, I'm not sure what will replace it.

You see, the fear of what is beneath it (even if it has the potential of being something good) is unknown. It isn't a hopeful "oh my gawd there's possibility there." It is more of losing a major part of yourself that you've known all your life. It is like losing your identity that you come to know all your life, even if the identity is twisted and not completely accurate.

See how difficult that could be to give this up? We all have these parts of ourselves. Even if they are parts we don't like about ourselves, they might have been there to help us survive situations, or get us through life. Without them, we may fear that we cannot survive or continue in life, even though that may not be the case. Survival in our early years has a tremendous impact on how we view our lives from that point forward.

This is part of the ego – the part that desires control, and feeds off our own energy. To allow this part of the ego to continue its neurotic feeding frenzy on us, aids in the denial of our true self. I'm not going to write that it is easy to let go, because I know from firsthand experience just how difficult this is, how much control the ego and these things have over us, and just how it can affect us physically.

As I went into the session, I came up against this part of me that did not want to let go. Was I successful that day in letting go? I'm not sure. I don't feel like I was, or I completely was at this point. In fact, it felt like a war was waging within me that day, from where Dr. Canali and his assistant, Quayny Porter-Brown, were trying to assist me in moving forward from the part that wasn't about to let go. He did some acupuncture on me that day, and the needle he had in my heart center (think that was what he called it) had to stay in for some time. He told me that my body was holding on to it for dear life.

The next day, I felt terrible in my body and I felt the anger full force. Fortunately I was able to work on myself on the table, and release some of this through my body. I feel much better now than I did the day after the session. A lot has moved through and out of me, which is good.

You know, I so badly want to flee from the effects of all that I've been through, and I wish I could wave a magic wand to do it. I know there is no such thing that exists, because the way through this is for me to go within myself, into and through the fear, and allow things to be let go. That's a process, and one that isn't necessarily easy. I'm just glad I could be honest that day with Dr. Canali about really being afraid to let go of these things, because I learned so much about myself that day. *(Written on 2/21/10)*

Throw The Garbage Out The Window

Until you clean out the closets, you cannot add anything to them.

Many schools of thought in spiritual circles and abundant living all talk about clearing out the old and making way for the new. Consider that springtime is a time of cleaning, and clearing out that which is old and no longer needed from the winter months. There is something to clearing out the old that just gives life and your surroundings a fresh start.

When I was young, my mother told me that a minister was talking about "throwing the garbage out the window" in a church service we attended. They thought it was cute when I got home from church, and I went around the house exclaiming, "throw the garbage out the window."

In our own lives, we need to do the same. It is nice to think positive thoughts, repeat affirmations, and make ourselves feel warm and fuzzy with all kinds of meditations each day. There is no harm in doing that, and it can help us reframe our mindset for the day. However, if we truly want to have those things, we must first get rid of the old. Without clearing out the closet of our life, there is no room for the new thoughts, the new affirmations, or the new positive concepts of abundance that we so badly desire.

Much like our physical bodies, as well, we need to get rid of the old to let the new in. Often we try to mask the pain through various medications, or even various types of bodywork. How many advertisements do you see for "pain management" out there? Take a look if you aren't aware of this, and you will see a lot.

Pain management only masks the pain. However, if you go into the pain and find its source (the emotional, biological, and mental connections), then you not only manage the pain, but more than likely you can let it go. By clearing out the pains of your life, you are clearing out the closets in your life. The more you clear out, the more you give your life, your mind, and your physical body room for greater awareness, peace, and a capacity to deal with the stresses of life.

Try to take note of the things you have in your closets; those things that you've shoved away in the closet and maybe don't even recall are in there. Just how much of your life is consumed by this, and is just taking up space? Take a close look. See all that is there.

Then work on cleaning out the closets in your life, including that of your physical body. For the more you do that, the more the closet will hold. This will reward you with so much more in life, and will give you a greater capacity to feel peace, calmness, and joy like you have never felt before. Yes, some of the things we find in our closets may be spoiled or ruined from the years of neglect, but thankfully we can "throw the garbage out the window." *(Written on 4/5/10)*

Putting A Puzzle Together

Okay, a show of hands – how many of you have put a jigsaw puzzle together? Ah, I see several of you have. So you will know firsthand what I am talking about. And for those of you who don't know, when you get done reading this article, take a trip down to the store and buy one! I actually bought one for my friend's birthday, which was a little risky because I didn't know how they would take this for a gift, but I thought it was a good idea and decided to take the chance. It turned out to be a very good idea, but that isn't the point.

It was a 550-piece puzzle of a beautiful stormy sea with the waves crashing against the shore, against the backdrop of a lighthouse. It really reminds me of a "safe and calm place" in the midst of stormy waters, a scene that really means a lot to my life.

Once the box was opened, we emptied all the pieces onto the table, and at once we noticed that many of the pieces had very similar colors, which meant this was going to be challenging. However, when faced with a challenge, you've got to figure out an action plan and then go for it, which is exactly what we did. The very first thing we focused on was getting the pieces of the frame put together, as once this was done, we could begin building all the pieces on the inside of the puzzle. Without the frame, it would have been a lot of fragmented parts here and there.

As the frame came together, we started to find groups of pieces that seemed to match each other, and as the hours went, we soon found the pieces that actually fit together. The more pieces we could put together, the more we could find major groups of pieces that went together. As this continued, the various parts of the puzzle began to take shape inside the frame. Soon we could begin to make out one part, then another part, and another until it started to resemble the picture on the box. With time, all of the pieces fell into place; even the pieces that seemed to fit more than one place in the puzzle. It wasn't too long before every piece had found its place in the puzzle, and the beautiful picture that resulted was just like the picture on the box.

As we completed this puzzle, I began to see the parallels between the activity, and how healing takes place in our lives. At first we may just see ourselves as a bunch of tissues and muscles that resemble a human. We may just look like a box with a pretty picture that only the outside world sees. As you open up the box and dump the pieces out, it looks like one big mess of junk, just like in our lives when we first start to confront our traumatic pasts, and begin down the road of healing. It looks like we are often times just a big bunch of pieces with nothing that fits together.

However, something miraculously happens! We begin putting one piece with another piece, and all of a sudden small parts of our life begin to form a picture. At that point, we might not be able to clearly see what the picture is, but we can see that there is something there. So we continue putting these groups of pieces together, and as we do, our shapes and colors begin to take dimension. We begin to see a little more of the bigger picture. However, we still may not be able to see the big picture of our lives, but we are definitely well on our way.

As we progress through our healing, our lives become less like a bunch of pieces sitting in a pile and more like a picture that shows who we are. With continued healing, we find more and more pieces that fit together, and fill in the missing holes of our lives.

Even though the road ahead may seem very difficult right now, if you just keep trying to put the pieces together, the picture will come together. The more you piece together or the more you heal, the clearer the picture will become. It does take time and it takes patience, but all you have to do is work with one piece at a time. The rest will take care of itself. *(Written on 7/03/03)*

Chapter Four

Rewiring The Brain

In the course of our lives, our brains become wired by the events we experience. While some events are welcomed, others need to be rewired.

<u>Selected Writings</u>

Rewiring The Brain

Surrender To Fear

David And Goliath Meet Fear

Fears In Perspective

Real Or Unreal

Allowing Things To Change

What Moves Us To Action?

We Need The Clouds

Affirmations

Rewiring The Brain

Consider for a moment that you are taking in billions of bits of information at every moment of the day. While our logical mind is unaware of that much information, it still makes an imprint on our brain. If we could stop a moment in time and analyze it, we would be amazed. And yet that very same information is sitting there waiting for us to tap into it and to give us insights which we would not otherwise have.

However, here comes the hard part. How do you get in touch with that part of you which you do not know about? Of course there are many different methods and pathways to get in touch with it, but one of the ways is through somatic awareness. Somatic awareness comes when we slow ourselves down far enough and allow our minds and our bodies to connect as one. Through this time, we merge what the mind knows with what the body senses, feels, smells, tastes, and touches.

If you touch yourself with a hot iron, your brain automatically senses the heat and makes a decision that this is not good for you, and you pull the iron back. You did not have to think about what hot meant and if this was good or bad for you. You did not have to think about whether you should pull the iron back from yourself and how to do this. It happened automatically. Your brain was "wired" to deal with the situation.

Now let's change this a little bit and let's say that you did this scenario every day. What would the result be? Most likely, what others would consider painful, you would consider a normal standard practice that really didn't cause any pain or discomfort. Others may look to you with utter shock as they witness you doing this, while you would be looking at it as if nothing mattered. In this instance, you've just managed to rewire your brain to accept something that is not something the body would normally accept without a degree of pain or discomfort.

So let's push this a little further and let's say you stop doing this to yourself. Of course as time goes by, you may develop complications in the area of the body where this was touched, but you ignore it for the moment thinking everything is okay. It is just a little pain or discomfort but nothing to cause alarm. After all, you have experienced something worse in the past than this. By this time, you've forgotten about the experience with the hot iron.

But of course as time goes, the pain and discomfort in the area continue to worsen, and soon those areas may not want to function or maybe a rash develops. Soon you realize that you have to get medical attention because this is limiting your daily functions in life, not to mention that it is becoming rather unpleasant to live with.

So after many tests are done, the medical establishment prescribes a drug that helps to take away the pain. While it helps momentarily, the effectiveness of the drug begins to wear off. You then decide to get further treatment which may include surgeries. They help temporarily, but again, the effects wear off. Your body continues to bring your attention to this area, and you keep searching for solutions outside of yourself to solve this problem when in reality, the cells of your body remember what happened to you.

Our cells remember so many things we experience. When there is pain or discomfort, these memories become embedded not only in our bodies, but in our brains as well. The stronger the emotions that coincide with these experiences, the more they are imprinted into our minds and locked there forever or until they are freed. Of course the cellular memories continue to try and resolve the situation moment after moment. The memories know there must be a way through this, and so they don't give up.

By this point, the mind and the body have taken over an experience and are now treating it just as automatic as breathing or having our heart beat. The body and the mind do not realize this is not operating outside of where it normally would be, because we have rewired the nerve pathways that connect these events. To our brain, this is a normal experience for our body, and to the body, it is just the way that it is.

Now let's surmise for a moment that we find a safe place with a safe person, and we begin to allow our body to sense whatever it is in that area that it can sense. At first, this may be next to nothing, but as we calm and slow ourselves down and we listen to that area of our body, we will begin to sense whatever it is that is showing up. The more we listen and connect with it, the more the brain begins to connect with that part as well. The more the brain connects, the more aware we become of something that was wired at a point in the past.

By listening, observing, and asking the body part what is going on without any judgment whatsoever, we begin to allow the cellular memories to complete the process they have been unable to take on. They are allowed to express themselves with all that was held in during the time the body part was going through these experiences. And if we continue to allow everything to show up fully and come out, then we finally free up all that was stored within our cells. It creates so much potential energy, because this is locked-up and stored-up energy that has had no place to go.

Of course, there may be a lot of tears, or fear, or all types of emotions that come out with this, but once we have allowed it to happen, we become freer than we had been before. We become more aware of so much more, and we connect our brains with our bodies in a very intimate and personal way. It becomes so freeing.

This, of course, was a very simple example. Imagine though what would happen if a child was beaten every time he tried to do something. Or maybe the child was yelled at every morning when he got up out of bed. What if maybe when a wife was fixing dinner, she heard her husband critique every little thing she did every day of their ten year marriage? What if you were driving along the road and someone blindsided you, or maybe some idiot cut you off and almost made you crash into the light pole? Or it could be something as simple as being stung by a bee as you were playing in your favorite playground. Think of how your body, your mind, your senses might have been at the moment of these events and then quantify those emotions that would most likely have been present. You can see just how strong of a combination this would be.

If these events were kept within the body with no way to exit, then they would become stored cellular memories with a lot of potential energy. That potential energy would work to find a way to release itself, and sometimes it finds a way that is not pretty. We've all seen people fly off the handle. We've all seen those road rage drivers, or the boss that walks into the office screaming at everyone in sight. We've all seen those silent moments when a person cowers in a corner trying to hide from the rest of the world. We've all seen the bullies on the playgrounds and in our everyday lives. Some people take it to extremes, walking into a crowded place and killing others. All of these and many more examples can be of potential energy trying to find a way out, trying to resolve itself, trying to release itself.

However, all too often, we ignore the signs and we do not listen to our bodies. We become desensitized to what it is that we actually feel is going on within ourselves. We shut ourselves down and we find ways to continue numbing ourselves, or self medicating ourselves. Then when things get too difficult, we look to doctors for the answers and they give us things that help for the moment. But we do not go to the root of the problem, the cellular memory of where everything originates. We ignore it and go for the easy fixes, even surgeries, hoping for resolution. And yet, we find no resolution.

Of course at some point in our life, the memory will get our attention and if we listen to it, we will have freedom and life but if we ignore it, our path will be difficult at best. It is a process of learning and connecting, then learning and connecting some more. Some experiences may be not as traumatic and they resolve much more quickly than others, while some may be so traumatic that we end up taking baby steps to resolve them.

And it is easy to want to do all of this healing work, focusing on the logical mind, but there is a cellular component that if left untouched, will not heal. There must be a release of both the cellular and the logical mind components to offer true healing. It does not matter what path you use to accomplish this, just that you do allow it to happen. *(Written on 9/25/07)*

Surrender To Fear

One of the biggest stumbling blocks to healing in my life comes by the vehicle of surrender. Fear, of course, throws up the wall, but surrender is the one drives through the wall. And yet, both of these affect my own healing and are stopping me from going into places where I need to go.

How many times do we say to others about situations we are going through that we are "fighting through this ordeal or problem or situation," or that sometimes things are just so difficult that we cannot find our way through them? We spend so much of our energy fighting so many situations, problems, and unknowns that we rob ourselves of so much possibility for our lives. Hey, I'm right there with everyone else on this because I do this as well.

Yet, so often we don't even realize we are doing this. It has become commonplace to us, in that we just see it as a normal part of our day or of life. We think that this is the way things are and always will be, and so we feel that we must fight head first into the winds that bear down upon us.

Recently, I kept getting reminded of surrender in my life. Sometimes my head is too hard to see it, and I've got to be taught a simple message, over and over again. While the message may be simple, our own consciousness holds us back from understanding it.

Consider when you go to bed at night and you have had a stressful day. You muscles feel tired, sore, and aching. Maybe you have a slight tension headache or other things affecting you. So you drop into bed, exhausted, and just thankful the day is over. Your eyes fall shut and you manage to drop into a deep sleep. That next morning happens to be the weekend, and it is a day that you can just sleep in and enjoy getting up very slowly. When you wake up, you realize that your body feels so much better than the day before and you feel more rested and refreshed. What caused the change? Most likely, it is that your body surrendered and let go of a lot of stress and tension that you went to bed with. I'm sure there could be other more detailed explanations, but for our simple example, this works.

If you have ever been on a massage table or in a Trager® session and you experienced the feeling of letting go, or just being there supported in time and space, then you will have experienced a degree of surrender. It is in that moment where we drop our guard down in a safe place, and at the hands of someone safe and trusted, that we give ourselves more freedom. Try to recall the feeling of what it was like before a bodywork session and what it was like after the session was over. Remember the difference? Remember how you felt once you surrendered? Lock that feeling in as a point of reference!

We can practice letting go in our mind by giving ourselves a moment throughout our day to do this. What if you sat there for a moment at your desk or in your job and just allowed yourself to let go of all that you were experiencing for that day? What would that feel like?

Another thing you can do is take one part of your body at a time and try to tense those muscles up as hard as you can. Then let them go. Try it a couple of times while really connecting and being present with what you are doing. It isn't time to think about everything else in your day. Just focus on this for a moment. Note the difference in your body, before and after. Can you feel a difference? Can you feel what more tense and less tense feels like? Notice the holding in your body and where it is located.

You might have just found places within you that you didn't realize were holding so much, or were as achy and tense as they are. When we go in and feel that which is there, we often notice so much more. That is the information our body is trying to feed back to us. It is biofeedback at its simplest moment. The more you are aware of your body, the more you are able to make decisions or changes about what you need to do for yourself. With an absence of information, our hope for change or improvement is diminished greatly.

In a recent session I had with Dr. Canali, I thought I had really gone far, in what I had done that day. To me, my body was feeling like it had gone as far as it needed to go. I didn't really feel a lot of tension or painful places at that moment, until I began to pick up on my shoulders being tight. It felt a little strange because it was not a normal pattern for me. As much as I tried to get myself to just let go – to surrender if you will – my shoulders remained tight and tense. It was almost as if the tension was increasing.

As Dr. Canali had me stretch my arms out front, he had them rest on a large foam bolster. He would roll my arms out, which of course stretched my upper arms and shoulders and then he would let them drop back (retract) into a moment of relaxation and surrender. The funny thing was, it was so difficult to let my arms and shoulders relax. And as we worked with this, I soon realized that my upper arm muscles and tendons were so tight and painful. I had never realized this before. Up until this point, I always thought my shoulder was the issue. It totally changed my perspective and my awareness on what was going on within my own body. Up until this point, I did not even recognize this state my muscles were in.

Of course, the surrender part was not easy. Even though I wanted to surrender and in my limited awareness of my mind, I was surrendering -- the pain stated otherwise. Just trying to get my shoulders to let go was really asking a lot. They held on for dear life, as if this was the only thing they knew how to do.

I'm not completely sure if I have connected all the dots yet, but I do know that one of my survival techniques throughout my early years was attempting to control everything around me. Most of the time, this was not realistic, but yet when you need to make sense of your world as it is filled with chaos, control is the only thing you can latch on to. Even if it is a false illusion, one tries to control and manage all parts of their life. It is dissociation between what is really going on in the mind and body, and what is actually taking place. It seems as real as it gets, but the truth is, there is a disconnect within us.

All of these things that I have described play into the tension we feel in life or the moments we are fighting against. Often if we stop for a moment and surrender into our fears, we will be propelled in the universe in ways we cannot even imagine. If we hold back and try to control all aspects of our life that we truly can't control, then we will be holding ourselves back from the possibilities that exist. It is all up to us of course. That means that we need to be aware of not only our thoughts in surrendering to fear, but we need to realize that our struggles against fear and surrender take up residence within our body. The more we can connect the surrender, fear, and our bodies together, the more we will propel ourselves forward. *(Written on 3/30/10)*

David And Goliath Meet Fear

For most of my life, fear has been one of my driving forces in all that I do, the decisions that I make, and the things that I choose. Fear is prevalent. It is everywhere and in everything and is often a part of us. However, the thing I'm learning in life is I can stand up and face the fear head on, and then let it go.

In my early days of therapy, I would remember my therapist asking me to "name" the fear that was coming up, and then we would talk through what is the worst thing that could happen. Once we did that, we would talk about what I could do if that happened. By doing this, I soon found out that most of my fears were just not as big and powerful as I thought they were. Yet, when you are looking at them face to face, they are often gigantic monsters.

Do you remember the bible story of David and Goliath? Where David took his little slingshot and a pebble and brought down the giant? Just think of fears in that way. They seem like they are bigger and more empowering than us, but all we need to do is use our little pebble of courage and determination to take them on. Once we decide to do this and let go of the fear that holds us, the giant falls to the ground.

Fear, though, can show up in so many ways, and often we do not recognize it. From the speeches of politicians, to the talking loudmouths of pundits on TV and the media doing their daily news reports, it is all filled with fear. Even the weather forecasts these days are fear based. Take a moment and think about this.

When you turn on the TV or whatever it is that you're listening to, you hear them talking about some issue, some concern or topic. And if you take a moment to look at it and see the "fear" behind what is being discussed, how does that impact you?

For example, let's say we turn on the TV and they are talking about some terrorist plot that is being cooked up, but they do not have concrete details, just that it might involve a football stadium or some other public place. What's your reaction? Do you get a twinge of unease within your body that maybe the football game you are going to could be the possible target of the terrorists? Most likely you do at some level.

Well, guess what? The media has been successful in instilling fear within you that you didn't have before you watched or listened to the program. I'm not saying you need to hide your head in the sand and be oblivious to what is happening in our world, but I am urging you to realize that most of the stuff is fear based. And if you don't believe me, put on your objective glasses and pay attention to what it is that you take in with your eyes and ears from the media and talking pundits in a day. Evaluate it and look at it. Don't just accept it.

Another source of fear is in the medical world of health, or what we perceive health to be. All of us have been through a moment where either our self or our loved ones ran up against a physical condition. What do we do first? Please be honest here. Let me repeat this: What do we do first?

We usually try to find something we can take to alleviate the pain, the condition, or situation. If we find nothing that works, then we head to the doctor. We may demand tests or medications or procedures to "cure" us of this condition. But if you take a moment and look within all that's going on, fear is alive and well. Fear feeds upon us and we feed upon fear. It fuels all kinds of biological conditions and most of us are oblivious that this is going on.

Yes, sometimes a doctor is needed to treat things. That's not the point I am trying to make here. The point is, when we come up against a biological condition in our bodies, let us first look within ourselves for the cause, instead of going into the fear that will only make things worse. If you do this, everything will be more different than you can imagine.

Fear can also show up as anger, where someone is so angry and they try to bite everyone's head off at every chance. They rule with control and they belittle anyone that tries to alter what is going on. They can be loud and boisterous, making sure that everyone hears them, or they can talk a mile a minute dominating every conversation. In the end, though, it boils down to the fear these people face. By using these different behaviors, it adds a layer of protection between them and the outside world. After all, if the fears of a person are great, it can be too much to connect with anyone around them in a meaningful and deep way.

Fear often has a way of keeping us from truly walking the path that we so deserve, and healing from those moments in life that were very difficult. It is much easier to paste a fake smile on our face, and try to convince the world around us that we have 'moved on' from all that we may have experienced. I know this is true because I've spent a lifetime doing it.

All of these things get locked up in the body. They are somatically a part of us, just as any body part is a part of us. While we try to separate the two, fear and somatic memory components are as much us as we are them. And while you're trying to convince the world around you that you have moved on, deep down within yourself (if you let yourself go there), you know that this isn't true. I completely understand just how difficult it is to stand up and grasp fear in your hands. It seems to be much easier to run away from it as fast and hard as you can, but in the end, fear will find you out.

There are so many ways fear shows up, and if we begin to keep an eye out for it, we'll start to see it. Fear is an energy drain and it robs us of so much in life. When fear builds up to a high level in our lives, we become overwhelmed and we either deal with it or it deals with us.

Yes, sometimes we can go for a long time and it seems like everything is fine but deep down, our body is hurting and getting ready to explode like a volcano.

We see this through aches and pains, weight issues, medical conditions, depression, anxiety, and so on and so forth. These conditions are a result of something in our body that needs to be healed, and something that we are hanging on to. It is the direct result of fear showing up and controlling our lives.

Waving a magic wand to get rid of it would be nice but there is no such thing. I get messages all the time about "products" or "healing methods" that allow you to bypass the fear. I have heard this so many times that I cannot even keep track of it. Yet each person, healing method, or product pusher is convinced that something they offer is the key to your well being. Unfortunately, there is no way around fear. The only way to do it is to go head first into it and take back the power it has robbed from your body. You can create the illusion for yourself that method or product "x" works, but if you're really and truly honest with yourself, you'll see the fear hiding deep in the shadows.

Again, I know it isn't easy to do this, but once you take that pebble and put it in your slingshot, you too can drop the giant, Goliath, to the ground. It may not be easy, or as instant as we are accustomed to, but it will be life changing and long lasting. Healing comes from that which you can feel in your body and connect with. It does not come from most methods, procedures, and products. The methods and procedures that have you totally connected with your mind and body, which allow you to go into the fear - now that's the way to heal! *(Written on 2/24/10)*

Fears In Perspective

Do you ever sit there and dream of wide blue sky and a world that you wish were your own? Do you ever make plans and begin on the path to accomplish those plans, just to be stopped right in your tracks? Do you have a strong desire and knowledge that there is just so much more out there for you, and yet it seems far beyond your reach? If this describes you, then you may be suffering from one of the same things I suffer from -- and that is fear.

Fear has ruled my life in so many ways, and just when I feel that I am naming the fears and overcoming them, up pops a new crop of fears along with the old ones. I've written so much about fear, and tried to find every way to put it into perspective that I could. I often find myself just wanting to rid myself completely of fear, and yet I know it is as much a part of life as joy, anger, happiness, and any other emotion. In fact, sometimes fear can be a lifesaver, or maybe just a kick in the seat of the pants that we need. However at times, fear can be overwhelming, and it can feel like it is getting the best of us.

As I was reading through a book, written by Oriah Mountain Dreamer called *The Invitation*, I noticed a section on fear. If you have never seen this book, I would strongly encourage you to find a copy, as it has so much insight into how we live our lives. One particular passage in the book on page 29, spoke to me in a very strong and deep way.

Here all along, I have been trying to chastise myself for being a wimp, for not being strong enough, and not doing enough to overcome the fears I have. It never occurred to me that the fear was a legitimate part of me, and that all I needed to do was to keep moving in the direction I had chosen to go. That sounds so simple to me right now, but in the past I have also done things the hard way, which robbed me of so many future rewards.

Maybe it is just a survivor trait that is in turbo mode, or maybe it is just part of who I am, but I think this is the first time I have understood that fear is as much a part of me as my arms or ears or eyes are a part of me. I do not need to worry about the fear nor do I need to expend the energy to nurture the fear. What I need to do is to choose the path I want to take, and then move in that direction. That is all I need to do; nothing more and nothing less. *(Written on 1/23/04)*

Real Or Unreal

What if how I looked at things that I thought were normal, real and in existence was in fact, not real? What if they were real today, but tomorrow they were not real because of what I could more readily see today? Our perspective, of course, changes each day, and so what we think is real today, most likely will look different tomorrow.

When I first thought about this, it made as much sense as some far out thought that just tries to confuse you. The more I've begun to unearth new things in my life, the more I see that this thought is indeed a valuable one. Let me give some examples.

Back in 2002, I decided to go to massage school. Considering I struggled pretty hard with anyone touching me (without being nauseated or numbing out), this was a monumental accomplishment for me. I still remember going for months in massage school struggling to feel the touch, and we basically had massages every day we were there. But now, because of that step, I was able to start going into other areas of healing for myself that I never dreamed possible. And before I moved to Florida, I would have never dreamed I'd be a massage therapist. Touch (giving or receiving) was the last place I'd ever thought I would find myself.

So what I thought was unreal [touch], now, for me, seems to be more real than what I believe to be real. Of course now, no touch seems to be unreal.

Another example is that of connecting with people in a way that I can be there with their pain, and not be overwhelmed. I've been working and training under Dr. Canali in somatic therapy based techniques. Some of the things that have been happening lately when I've been there (ever since my own energy healing session) have surprised the both of us. And I never ever thought I would be connecting with people the way I am, nor would I have thought I could be there as the pain of past events surfaced (and not be afraid).

So what I thought was unreal - connecting with people - now, for me, seems to be more real than what I believe to be real. Of course now, not connecting with people seems to be unreal.

A more personal example is at one time I didn't think I could ever be in a relationship, let alone a gay relationship. I wouldn't allow myself to honor the gay part of myself, because I had been taught just how "evil" being gay was and that I'd be going to hell for it. A very important side note: In my life, I've already been to hell and back, so I guess that carrot of fear just doesn't work with me. But I never thought I could be with someone, truly love them, and long to be with them. I never thought I could be intimate with them not only in sex, but in emotions, feelings, and the mind/body/soul aspect. And yet Jeff and I have a very strong love between us that continues to grow each day, and we are growing not only as a couple but as individuals as a result.

So what I thought was unreal - relationships - now, for me, seems to be more real than what I believe to be real. Of course now, no relationship seems to be unreal.

Another more personal example is that I never thought I would fully recover from the effects of being paralyzed, from anxiety, from depression, from my nervous stomach/ulcer, from the stiffness that my body feels on a daily basis, and from migraine headaches I've suffered all my life. And then I met Dr. Canali, and so much has changed in my life. Things that I thought were going to be a part of my life forever are slowly disappearing. I've met some wonderful people online that have helped me in my quest for understanding, for answers. I've discovered a new bodywork method called "Trager®" that is allowing my body to understand touch more and to integrate a more free movement and oneness in myself.

So what I thought was unreal - understanding and healing - now, for me, seemed to be more real than what I believe to be real. Of course now, no understanding, no healing, or no hope seems to be unreal.

For me, the paralysis is a constant reminder to go further, to take steps, to have the courage to face the impossible. There isn't a day that goes by that I am not thankful that I can get up out of bed, and walk, talk, move, take care of myself. And the determination that I had to walk again has fueled me to keep going, to keep healing, and to keep trying to discover what is out there. I could have easily given up many years ago, and I could have easily just accepted all that I was enduring as it was going to be the way it was. However, I said no to all that, and fought my way back from hell.

Now even as I am healing in deeper ways in my own life, I'm once again reminded what was unreal is becoming real to me now. I'm beginning to see that I have a higher purpose in life. I always thought because of what I went through in life, that there was no chance of me recovering and partaking in the beauty of life. But as I heal, I'm beginning to see new mountain peaks that I never knew existed. It doesn't mean it is easy and it has been a very difficult journey so far, but the view is more and more breathtaking every day. And as I look at my life now compared to a time not long ago, I can see there is hope, there is healing, and most of all there is life! *(Written on 1/25/05)*

Allowing Things To Change

Sometimes I want things to change in life so badly. My fears try to get the best of me, and self confidence falls to an all time low. I am constantly reminded, though, that all of this is part of my journey. I need to allow it to unfold and let the prompts in life guide me.

Allowing is difficult to do in life. For when things seem so noisy and stressful, you just want to move through them as quickly as you can. However, it is most likely the same as the song Garth Brooks sings, "I could have missed the pain but I'd of had to miss the dance." It is part of the process, no matter how difficult the process may become.

Of course, the frustration, pain and discomfort are messages of prompting to help find our way. They are like bumper railings in life. Sometimes, though, it is easy to focus on the bumps and not on the path.

It takes courage, determination, and staying open to all that we experience. What we may see today that makes no sense in this moment, may be the cement we use to build tomorrow's bricks for our path. *(Written on 7/19/10)*

What Moves Us To Action?

What moves us to action? Is it our fears, our longings, our passions, or desires? Could it be that others are responsible for moving us to action? Maybe it is an event, a person, or some place that we travel to, that prompts us to do something.

There are times that it is hard to explain, but we know deep down inside of us that there is something we must do. We feel it in ways that are clearly evident to us. Often times, we feel as if we stand alone as we prepare to take action, all the time knowing, we must do this.

It is often scary and unknown. There is usually no road map or a detailed list to guide our way. Sometimes, even the objective is unclear at the moment we start. For us to look forward, it can be unimaginable how far this path of action will lead us.

While it can be easy to feel discouraged by the fear and worry of the unknown, we must remember to stay in the moment of now. We may not see how individual and unconnected points fit together as they come by. It may be some time before we can view how all parts of our life moments fit together into a beautiful story.

We should never cease to dream, or fail to live our dreams. For through the dreams, we open ourselves up to all that is possible. By opening ourselves up, we find that which excites us. Honoring that which excites us moves us to action. It is at that point, where we truly find our feet on our path. *(Written on 7/15/10)*

We Need The Clouds

Sometimes in life, our hearts come upon moments that can be challenging and difficult. We may have lost someone dear to us, or may just be struggling as we hit the speed bumps in life.

While it would be nice to have only days of sunshine in our lives, we do need the clouds and the rain. Imagine what the world would look like without clouds and rain. It is the same in our life. It allows us to compare and contrast feelings, emotions, and experiences. Being able to compare and contrast gives us the opportunity not only to experience sorrow, but recognize when happiness is around us. One without the other would leave us unbalanced.

Yes, it can be difficult to deal with the rough moments in life. Sorrow feels draining and never ending at the time we are experiencing it. However, if you look back on those difficult moments in your life, you hopefully will notice that you made it through them. Even though at the time it felt like you were being pulled under, you did make it. You made it through with flying colors.

It does not mean that these times were easy or short in duration. It just means that through your creative wisdom and personal discovery, you found a way beyond them. Often it is the darkest just before the dawn. So too, is it sometimes the most difficult before we realize just how much we are growing.

Sometimes life is harder to understand while you're looking at one individual moment. However, if you can widen your viewing angle, you may very likely be surprised at just how it changes. It took very little effort on your part just to see what was happening, even in the midst of the difficult moment.

May we have eyes that can never close. May we have a desire to be more than we are today. May we allow ourselves to reach deep within for the energy, the strength and the courage we need in life. And may we give thanks for each and every experience in our lives. For without them, we would not be who we are today. *(Written on 7/18/10)*

Affirmations

An affirmation is a statement in present tense that is positive and helps us move toward our goals. It is stated in a manner that is assertive and as a declaration, as if it is something that has already happened.

I remember back to the days that I struggled to think anything positive about myself, which was preventing me from going outside and being around people. I did not like myself, and you could probably even say that I hated myself during this time. I did not see any value, just ugliness from my past. No matter how much I talked about this in therapy, it just didn't seem to make a difference. Regardless, I had myself convinced that I was nothing, I was dirty, ugly, and responsible for everything that had happened to me. It was a self-fulfilling prophecy and the more I believed it, the more it became me. So what did I do? Read on.

Shaina Noll has a CD called *Songs For The Inner Child* with a song on it titled, "How Could Anyone". For lyrics and more information, go to the following link: http://mindbodythoughts.blogspot.com/2009/06/how-could-anyone.html.

What I did for a month was listen to this song by Shaina Noll, over and over. I would play it in the morning before I went to work, and when I got home from work. I would listen to the song and usually try to sing it, since no one else was around to hear me.

But after the month went by, I found that for the first time I started believing that I was worth something, and how could anyone ever tell me that I was anything different than that? Once I started believing this and letting it sink into my life, I started to change. That was the point where I once again began to venture out around people and beyond the four walls of my fortress I called a home. From that point on, my life has taken a new course that has led me to discover many new oceans, some of which right now are a direct result of this time.

As we were talking about affirmations in my class at Educating Hands School Of Massage, I realized that I have been doing this a lot through my healing. I've created affirmations for myself and used them to help me go places where my logical, afraid self could not go. So many times when fear paralyzed me from taking a step, the affirmation would go before me. Just think in your mind for a second how powerful that could be. You don't have to be any special writer or talented person to do this. All you have to do is let yourself be you, and focus on what you want for your life.

In class we were all asked to create an affirmation for ourselves. I still struggle hard with having the confidence in life to do what I need to do, and while it has improved, I get so scared at times and would love to be more confident.

So my affirmation was "I AM CONFIDENT". Yes, I don't feel that way right now but I continue to repeat this to myself each day, and before long, it will be the direction my body will be going. Because the more I tell myself that I am confident, the more my body will take on the necessary skills, qualities, and resources to be confident.

Take a moment right now as you are reading this, and think about an affirmation for yourself. Maybe you have too much debt, and the affirmation could be "I am wealthy." Or maybe you are a couch potato and want to be fit as a fiddle. The affirmation could be "I am healthy", or "I am physically fit." Maybe you struggle with hating yourself and your affirmation could be "I love myself." The possibilities are enormous and as wide as the widest ocean. The power lies within you, and all you have to do is turn the faucet and tap into it.

An affirmation should be something that is a simple statement. That way you can remember it easily, and repeat it without much effort or thought. It should be a statement of positive thoughts and words. For instance, if you are in debt, you would not want to use the phrase "I want to be debt-free" because your mind would still be focusing on the debt, which is not a positive thought. Instead, "I am wealthy" would be a more positive statement.

Make sure your affirmation is personal to you, and make sure you can own it. Once you've created it, try to find a safe person that you can share it with, because the power of the words will be multiplied many times over. And once you've done all of this, then start repeating it to yourself every day until it becomes you and you become it. Allow your affirmation to change your life in whatever way it is needed.

You know I often struggled through my healing, with wondering where the answers were for many of the things that I faced, or how I should heal, or what things I needed to do to heal. But I am finding more and more that all of the time, the answers were right inside of me. They were already a part of me. Your body knows what you need, and by tapping into the strength and wisdom each of us has, we can grow and soar in ways that will amaze us. *(Written on 10/10/02)*

Chapter Five

Personal Growth

To grow and evolve as humans is one of the greatest gifts we can give ourselves. To grow and evolve is to be human. It is our spiritual connection.

Selected Writings

Ask The Question

Keep It In Perspective

Ignore The Pain

Reflections On My Life

Balance For The Mind And Body

Illusion Or Reality

Release It, Let It Go

Enjoy The Symphony

Your Choice To Awareness

When Life Is Too Busy

Ask The Question

When I took my Trager® training, one of the main things we were taught was to "ask the question". What do I mean by that? I'm glad you asked the question!

An example in body work is when you're working with someone's shoulder, and it isn't letting go. You've tried just about every trick that your anxious brain can think of at that point and nothing is working. So one of the best things to do is silently "ask the question" to yourself. It could be anything from "what do you need?" to "how can I be here for you?" to any number of questions.

And we are taught that when we ask the question, we wait for the answer and listen to the answer because it will appear. You may not see it directly or you may, but it will show up if you allow it.

Along with that, sometimes, is just being there, and "holding the space" open for the person. Sometimes the body doesn't need for you to do anything to it. It just needs someone to be there with it in an unconditional way, doing nothing and attempting to do nothing.

All of this applies to our individual lives, and in fact, our everyday lives. How many times do we come up against things in our day where we're not sure of how to proceed? How many times do we face obstacles in our life, that we have absolutely no idea what it takes to get beyond? How many times do we feel we face mountains so high we don't even know where to get started?

See where I'm going? Okay, if you don't that's fine, and I'll explain where I heading with this. If we have no idea how to even have hope for the situation we're in, we could always ask a simple question, "How do I have hope?" or "How do I get beyond this obstacle or mountain?" It doesn't have to be these questions, as you can come up with your own, and that way it works better for you. Sometimes when I've been screaming and crying from what seems like no way out, some of the best questions come forth. The important part though is to ask the question. Ask "how things might be different?" Ask "what is possible or what could be?"

But don't stop there - - when you ask, allow the answers to come through. Try not to put a blindfold on, while proclaiming you want to see the answer. Try not to evade the answer even though it is chasing you down the street. Try not to mold the answer or answers into your preconceived ideas of how things should be. We all do these things but when you ask, allow the answers to come just as they are, in their own way and in their own time. The answers could be very subtle, and so if you're not looking, they might slip in the door before you realize it. That's fine if you don't see them slip through the door, but try not to miss them either because they are very special to us.

You may end up asking the same question every day for many days and that's fine too, because it may be the way you are helping your mind focus on what it needs. Remember we create what we want in our life, and if we are in the question, then we are creating what we want.

So if you're up against one of those things in your life that just seem to confuse the dickens out of you, take a moment right now and think about what question you can ask that fits the situation. Keep the question simple and then allow it to come through to your life.

Last but not least, enjoy the answers that you receive, even if they don't appear to be the ones you were trying to anticipate. *(Written on 11/14/08)*

Keep It In Perspective

Sometimes life can throw them at you hard and fast, and if you don't duck quickly enough, you get slammed in the face! Really, it can! I know many of you probably already know that. Sometimes, though, it just feels like a tidal wave or a hurricane has slammed ashore in your life.

In the past week, I've been hit several times with some major stressors and each one stung a lot. All of the situations were out of my control, yet they impacted me directly and with gusto! Different people, different frameworks and different situations lined up and attacked at once it seemed. Believe me, at one point I was ready to run for cover, yet there was no place to run.

I tried to deal with each situation as best as I could, but the accumulation effect began to make the little things grow into much bigger things. One event hit me so hard that it really made me extremely angry. The minute I felt the anger, I was literally feeling the need to vomit my guts out. A headache raged on, and my abdomen was so bloated that moving around or sitting was excruciating. For the rest of the night and into much of the next day, I physically didn't think I was going to make it. And of all days, I had a task to perform that went almost 15 hours from beginning to end. So now, I'm not only dealing with the anger and physical ills but I'm feeling exhausted, stressed, tired, etc.

Yet, I am listening to my body and hearing it say to me that I need to stop, regroup and hit that reset button. So here's what I'm doing.

1) The things that I can take care of, and what I need to do, I'm working on. If it is beyond my control, I'm just trying to say it isn't my concern for now and I have to trust the system in place.

2) On things that needed immediate attention for me to stand up and be accounted for, I had conversations with the person stating to them that their way of doing business was a very bad practice. After all, I lost a serious amount of business income because of a decision they made that strongly impacted me. While they didn't like me confronting them and it may impact further income, I had no choice really, because they would have just walked all over me in the future.

3) The things that were just too consuming and toxic at the moment had to be put off. After all, I can only do and deal adequately with so many things at one time. I've learned that I don't have to solve everything with others at one moment. Sometimes we need to regroup and reassemble in order to move forward. That's what I'm doing.

4) I'm trying to take time off and just rest and give myself some downtime. While I can't just run off and get away from phones, email, and other responsibilities, I can limit myself for a day or two. My body is screaming for the rest and is hitting the reset button whether I like it or not. So I've got to follow what my body wants, or there will be hell to pay!

5) I plan on getting the creative side of me out and just allowing myself to bask into the calmness and groundedness and centeredness of it all. Allow myself to go in to that place that is peaceful, calming and soothing, and to connect with the higher side of myself.

Sometimes perspective on stresses and issues in life is very difficult to keep. Sometimes we get so bombarded like in a game of dodge-ball that we have to find a corner to hide in or catch the balls coming at us. Whatever we do, there are times when we really just need to stop and find a way to catch our breath, regroup, and hit the reset button.

If you're stressed and feeling bombarded, it is time to take a moment and do a reset in life. Don't keep trudging through everything because you think you have to. If you stop and rest a little, you'll fuel your body back up to take on everything coming at you. If you exhaust yourself, you will be taken out by the dodge balls! *(Written on 4/23/10)*

Ignore The Pain

How far am I willing to go to ignore pain?

One of the things I have been thinking about lately through the tooth pain is just how much I ignored it. I really didn't think I was ignoring the pain, but as I look back, I realize that I was. An intense pain that would not give up was pushing me into actually doing something about it. Imagine the depths I went to just to avoid the inevitability of going to the dentist.

At first, I was having a painful wrist, where it was hard to do anything with my right hand. I was trying to explain it in my mind as carpal tunnel, or spending too much time using the mouse on my computer. Little did I realize at the time, my body was compensating for me during my sleep time at night. It was helping me to avoid lying on the side of my face that hurt, by using my hand to shield me from the pain. I was completely oblivious that this was going on. Yet, I felt the wrist pain.

Then there was the sore throat and the barely felt tooth pain, which I just passed off as heat stress and allergies from yard work. However, the tooth pain and pressure in my jaw persisted days after these stresses. Yet, I did not allow myself to connect with the pain. I was oblivious to it.

Even in the days leading up to the start of the horrible tooth pain, I tried to ignore the nuisance of it. I remember using ice packs on my mouth to help relieve the pain. This was all done in silence and away from the view of house guests we had staying with us.

I could not let anyone know the truth about how bad the pain was. If I did, then everyone would have seen the shame that I harbored deep within me, I reasoned. I didn't want anyone to see that. The shame I felt from being triggered to things in my past was nothing I wanted anyone to know about. I suffered in silence, hoping that all of this would just go away.

The thing is, the pain got so intense that I had to push through the fears and shame to make an appointment. I was so scared to call the dentist office that I sat with the intense pain for many days. For in my mind, it was not about the tooth that needed attention. It was about the shame that it connects to, that my mind so badly wanted to hide from. While that may sound "strange", it is at the root of what is behind my avoidance of the dentist.

Just imagine, though, what my mind and body was willing to do to avoid the pain and not deal with it. They did everything they could to pretend the pain was not there. My body completely disconnected from the pain. It found ways to compensate and shift the pain to other areas, but it was still there. It tried to cover it up and act as if it did not exist.

We all do this in our lives to one degree or another. It may be back pain, neck pain, illness, disease, colds and flu, headaches, financial stress or just about any other situation we face in life. If this sounds too farfetched, read any one of Dr John Sarno's books and see what the body connects to and how far it is willing to go. Times of pain, discomfort and frustration in our lives, are the ways in which our body, mind, and spirit try to get our attention.

It is wise that we listen to these messages from the body and not ignore them, for they show up for a reason. They help us grow, heal, move forward, and evolve our lives. If we medicate them or compensate for them, we may alleviate the pain and discomfort temporarily, but they are still there. Not until we go in and deal with these things, will we get to the true source of the pain.

It will be like a tiger waiting in the brush, ready to pounce upon its prey at an unexpected moment. The slightest trigger or unrelated event may begin a cascade of situations that once again bring us front and center with our pain. May we then have the courage to embrace and allow it, instead of compensating and running from it. For when we embrace courage, we truly give ourselves the moment to change our lives forever. *(Written on 7/9/10)*

Reflections On My Life

I've been doing a lot of thinking lately and realizing just how far I've come. Maybe that's the message I was looking for recently when I felt like I was up against the same proverbial brick wall. It was a familiar brick wall, and one that seems to be there no matter what.

You see, my life has been deluged with many storms. I've been battered in just about any way one can think of that a person can be. There haven't been too many things that I've not encountered in my life in one way or another. Some people have told me that I chose this life, which at first was hard to reconcile, but the more I challenge and look at what these people have told me, the more it makes sense. I was never one to believe in past lives, but too many things have surfaced that give evidence that there is more out there than what I was taught in some narrow-minded churches.

When I was a kid, I never really thought I would make it through high school. I always just knew "somehow" that I was going to get very sick and the entire family would be around me wondering what to do. No one would have answers and it was a life threatening situation. As a kid, I thought this would happen before I graduated from high school but instead, it was a few years after I was out of college. And while I couldn't see the entire manner in which this would play out, it did involve my family wondering how to get me the help I needed, and the doctors being unsure of what to do. Fortunately I did recover but it was a very difficult moment in my life, and I did come very close to death.

All the while growing up, though, I was an extremely sensitive kid. I'd cry at anything and everything. If I was separated from my mom, I'd cry. If I saw some little creature on the ground tortured or mistreated or even stepped on, I would cry. I had a pet rock and if someone would hit it, I would cry. There were people around me that could not accept that, and being a boy, I was taught to be a "man" and not cry. Of course, this just made me go and hide my head under a pillow and cry myself to sleep. The point is I was very sensitive and I picked up so much that was around me -- from what people were thinking and not saying, to how they felt, how they responded to me and so many other things. It was like I was acquainted with a language that was not spoken or shared. Of course, my home life was not a stable, grounded life, and so these things became misdirected as self sabotage for me. That led to stomach and digestive problems, headaches, self confidence issues and so many other things because I internalized everything.

By the time I reached high school, I knew I was just different than others, or they were just different than me. I didn't feel like I fit in, nor did I really want to. Many things I knew seemed to evade others, and I was often confused that concepts which I understood were so far removed from most of the population. I still struggle with that to this day, because somehow I just understand things and I have no idea where they came from.

Today, I still struggle with self confidence and feeling like I fit into life. There are concepts which just seem normal to me, but 99.9% of the population just doesn't get them! And they don't seem that concerned either.

I'm still very sensitive and really learning that this is a good thing in my life, but sometimes it is overwhelming, to say the least. Sometimes walking in a store with a lot of people, is a major challenge for me. It is as though everyone has their own life's movie playing around them as they walk by. Sometimes, I pick up the pains that these people have, and then struggle to figure out if they are my pains or another person's pain.

Some days I still feel really out of place in this life, and sometimes I have no way to reconcile that with anything. It is hard to find well rounded, grounded people to talk to, because so many go out into all forms of la la land and they can't even see that they are in la la land. I'm learning, though, that all of these things are helping me grow into the person that I am. While I want everything to come together in life, and know exactly what I'm supposed to be doing and what it is I feel I'm being groomed for, I know that until the moment is right, there will be the feeling of a void. My sense and message is that all of this is taking place quicker than I realize, but it is not time yet.

Why did I write this? I'm not sure. It may just be my way of trying to connect the dots. It may be my way of showing me that this is going along as planned, or it may be a whole host of other reasons. Whatever it is, my hands felt the need to write my thoughts down, and I'll let the words go wherever they may travel.

It is my quest to understand more about my life, to heal from the storms of life, and to follow that inner guidance within myself that shows me the path ahead. *(Written on 4/01/09)*

Balance For The Mind And Body

Balance is so very important to our lives, and yet it is easy to be knocked or pulled in certain directions in life. Whether it is noise in our day, pains we must face, or having to determine what our priorities are, we all are influenced by these things.

If you notice, though, there are people who are able to stay the course. They know the route they need to sail and so nothing veers them off course.

Then there are others that are tossed to and fro, as the waves of life batter their ship. The waves don't have to be very strong either. They hold on for dear life, hoping that only smooth waters are in the future. Yet, they forget that the wind not only propels them, but also creates the waves. It is hard to have one without the other.

So how do we deal with life when it seems to be more in control, with us as willing participants? Maybe if we stopped each day and gave ourselves a moment of pause, we would clear our minds to put our day in a different view. What if instead of trying to mask the pains we felt, we looked for the courage to allow them to speak their messages to us? What if we held our moments of quietness in the same regard and emphasis as we do our busy moments?

Yes, it may be true that this could lead us to changes in our lives. It may push us to rethink our priorities in any given day. It all depends, of course, on what gets our attention in our day and what we choose for our lives.

Our bodies send us messages through pain, when we fail to listen to them. Our lives send us discomfort, when we are stepping off into the edges of our path. When we run from our fears, questions of what we should do, and moments of confusion hold us from embracing the courage that we need.

In the end, all the answers we need for our life can be found within us. While others may help us to discover our truth we hold inside of us, it is our self and our body that holds the answers. We will not find them anywhere else. It is up to each one of us to be open, to listen, and to allow the messages and wisdom we hold, to come forth. All too often we stifle the message and curse the messenger.

It sounds so simple but sometimes fear makes us think we have a giant to conquer. However, if we stuck a tiny pin into the giant, it would deflate instantaneously.

May each of us examine our life and embrace our own messages, as we find our courage to put the pin into the giant of our fears. May each of us not run and hide, but fully embrace every little part of our lives and our bodies. For the more we become one with ourselves, the more united we are. So when the winds of life blow on our sails, we will be strong and secure. We will be at one with our life and who we are as an evolving and growing consciousness. *(Written on 6/30/10)*

Illusion Or Reality

I see and hear so many people in this world screaming at the top of their lungs. Often, it is about politics or religion or some injustice in the world. While these are noble causes that usually involve passion, emotion, and action, they tend to be more extreme than they need to be.

Take notice of the way many things are displayed in the news. Or how about the format in which movies are created and entertainment is participated in. How about the activities we connect to? Everything seems to be bigger, greater, more dramatic, and more extreme. Now we even have 3D to enhance movie viewing. It is as if we cannot get enough or that we've set the bar so high that now we need more stimulation in life.

Let's go back to the people screaming, or should I say in modern terms, "people discussing things in life and social networking and the news." If you look past the screaming, you'll notice that no one is truly listening or respecting what others have to say. Opinion is now shrouded as fact. Sensationalism is portrayed as energy and passion. Whoever can out talk, out yell, or out last their fellow human (aka opponent), is deemed the winner in that moment of life. Of course, the moment changes rapidly these days and so the winner today, may be the loser tomorrow.

To me, this is a sad testament to not only our individual existence, but the universal connections we share. It is easy for many of us to judge, critique, and get caught up in viewing the world through those that excite and motivate our passions, as we tend to see them currently in our lives. In many ways, we are no different than those we judge or embrace. We are as much a part of the screaming as they are.

Yet, how far is this getting us in life? Is it solving problems or truly making us more enlightened? Is it helping us to grow individually and collectively as humans?

While escapes from everyday stress and pains can often bring relief, we need to identify it as such and not live life as an illusion. The screaming, judging, and need to have more sensationalism in our lives is an illusion. It is a mask for what we truly feel in our lives, or the things we would rather not feel. Of course, this is old news to most people because deep down, we know this already in our mind, body, and spirit.

Maybe instead of trying to prove or disprove how much each of us participates in the network of illusion, we may want to play the role of observer. Try taking the next day or week, and observing what input you take into your life. I'm not asking you to set yourself apart from the world, just to observe and notice.

Ask yourself, what is the purpose? What is it that I get from this? Then if you're bold enough, you may want to consider if you really need that input, or could you replace it with something that connects you more with your mind and body, offering much greater rewards to yourself.

Sometimes it isn't easy taking a good hard look at our lives. We feel that we have to follow along like everyone else. The funny thing, though, is how collectively we are learning to live reality as an illusion. It is all around us if we just take a moment to look at it. We can fool ourselves and explain or rationalize the illusion in many ways, but in the end, it is still an illusion. *(Written on 7/08/10)*

Release It, Let It Go

Often there are times in my daily life when I just struggle to let go of things. I give lip service that I actually do let go, but if I was honest, I would have to own up to not letting go completely. Even if I manage to let go of most of the situation, usually I still cling to a part. Sometimes, that is a small part, but it truly says I did not release it and let it go.

It could involve situations that happen online, or through communication with people I know. It may be experiences with people in public places, or in work situations. Often it involves financial stress and worry, such as paying the bills. In all of these circumstances, I observe myself worrying, holding it in, and clinging to that which I cannot control.

While the illusion of control probably gives nourishment to my mind, it seems never to be in short supply. Although I have made great strides in working through this, I know that to release situations in life and let them go, is not easy. I'm not saying it is impossible but it has taken much work to get as far as I have gotten.

It does seem that I continually forget that I am not in this world alone. I have help, support, and love from people around me, as well as the angels. I've been a witness many times to all of this and yet, I still try to face life on my own. I act as if I am in a void apart from everyone, and as if I have to go it alone.

While I know control issues date back to prehistoric times in my life, they are not healthy and balanced for me. I can feel the control, worry, and stress build up in my shoulders, neck, and back. It robs me of precious energy in my day and alters how I view my life. As much as I want to let go of the control, I find myself attracted to it as a tempting and seductive desire. It is like I allow it to be chained to my neck as I attempt to drag it through my life.

The question then becomes, how do I let it go? How do I release it? I would think that I first need to recognize when I'm not giving up control. Unless I know that control is in play, how would I be able to give it up?

The next part of this would be to acknowledge it and allow it to be there with me, so that I can learn what it is that I need to learn. By keeping myself in the observer mode, it may have a great deal of wisdom to share with me. By allowing it to be in the current moment, I have now taken the power back from it. I have empowered myself instead of being manipulated by it.

The final step would be to find out why I wish to hold on to this moment. What is in it for me? When I can truly be in this space of awareness and the current moment of now, then I will have the option to let go and release it.

With the help of the angels and the support and love of people around me, I will find the energy boost to do this. It will be the ultimate spark to allow this to happen. It will allow me to remember the magical sense of wonder in life, and to embrace it fully. *(Written on 7/10/10)*

Enjoy The Symphony

When we listen, what do we find? That can be an earth shattering, mind numbing question, or it can be one of joy. As always, when you are attempting to listen, you will discover things that have always been there, but that you were not aware of readily.

Take, for example, something I'm sure you do every day. As you walk outside to your car or to get a newspaper or to go to work, what do you hear? I bet if you had to write down every sound that was going on around you, your mind would be mostly blank. Or you might be able to record a few things that you hear, but so many other sounds would go unnoticed.

Let's take this one step further. What if you said that you heard the birds singing in the morning as you got into your car? That would be a lovely thing for you to connect with, but still one deeper question remains: Exactly what do the birds sound like? How loud are their chirps? In what manner do they make sounds? Are they high or low pitched, long or short, whistling or single syllable? Why is this even important, you might ask right now?

The reason it is important is that to connect fully with the bird singing, you need to be fully present. Just hearing a bird chirp on a passing day doesn't necessarily connect you intimately to that situation. It means you just notice the sound and you're in a hurried pace of life going to your next scheduled task.

Of course, we can't spend every minute of our day tracking all the sounds around us, and that is not the point of this discussion. The point is that when we listen, we find more! When we observe, we see more. When we ponder, we understand more. When we ask, we are given so much more. However, if we continue in our hurried pace of life every day, then when do we have time for all of this? We only wish and hope that we discover, learn and receive, when in fact we are often standing in the way of what is all around us. It isn't something out there way beyond us in the blue clear sky. It is right next to us. It is within us. It is part of us! It is us!

So try this out. Take a moment and step outside and just listen. Focus on nothing more than that. Once you've done that, try to capture what you've just heard through some creative means. Therein lies the joy of listening and discovering and just being out of our hurried pace in life. Therein lies the experience of life and all that it possibly can be, as you focus not on a life of scheduled events, but one of being connected to something much greater than you could ever imagine.

Enjoy the symphony!
(Written on 7/03/08)

Your Choice To Awareness

We are what we are in life, and we are what we have not dealt with in our lives. While that may sound complicated, it is really a simple statement.

All of your sum experiences up until this moment in life have made you the person you currently are. All the good, bad, ugly, beautiful, and even the forgotten moments come together and have created you as a person, a soul, and an entity.

In addition to this, the unconscious or conscious choices we have made not to deal with all aspects of our lives are a part of who we are as human beings living in breathing, physical bodies. Yes, there are many things that we choose not to become aware of, just as there are many unconscious things of which we're not aware.

So often, though, I've run into people of all ages and walks in life that paste the happy, "I'm past these things" smile on to their face. They proclaim that the best way forward is to just not think about the past and move on. They hint that you just have to focus your attention on the present and what lies ahead, while you forget all that took place which may have been unpleasant.

Often you will hear these people say "just put your past behind you," or "you just need to move on. I've moved on, why can't you?" You might even hear things like "quit living in the past," or "you just need to pick yourself up and move on," or "get over it or just move on." There are a number of things that get said, and most of these statements reflect more upon where that individual stating them is in their own life, rather than what you need to do.

Many of us may have been given a horrible hand in our past to deal with, and there is no way at this moment in our lives that we can go back and change that. What happened to us is part of us, whether we want to own it or not. On the other hand, if we do not deal with all that happened, then we are playing with a ticking time bomb.

Yes, all of these things will continue to eat away at us through the following: anger; relationship issues and problems; excessive indulgences like drinking, smoking, drugs, work, etc., and difficulties in many areas of our lives. If we continue to let these things fester and find a home in our lives, they will become a ticking time bomb that will go off at some point. How it goes off will vary by the person, but it is almost guaranteed that it will.

So is this a life sentence? No! It does not have to be unless we allow it. I know I hear you saying, "Well it's not fun or easy or pretty to deal with." I hear some saying as they are reading this that "I've got better things to do with my time than to deal with all of this stuff that I'd just rather forget." I hear some saying that "you just don't know how hard I had it in my life."

Unfortunately, I do know how difficult it can be in life, and I've been through so much in my own life. Yes, we can choose not to deal with it because it is too tough, or difficult, or too ugly, but then we are truly robbing ourselves of what it really means to be human. We are affecting everyone around us that we interact with, and we are affecting the entire population and the universe as well. We don't just rob ourselves of all that can be. We rob the entire universe of being all that we can be.

It is a choice we make, whether it is a conscious or unconscious one. To make no choice at all means we are sticking with the status quo in our lives, and choosing not to become all that we are meant to be. It is as simple and complicated as that. We have the power to make the choices for our lives that we desire, and we also have the power to free ourselves from the fear, the pain, and horrors of our past whether we feel like we do or not.

It is up to each one of us to make the choice of what we will do with the hours we have today. It is up to each one of us whether we will remain unconscious in our awareness, or if we will consciously choose to become aware of all that we are. No one else can do this for us, and no one else can make the choice. Yes, it does take others to help you walk through some of these troubled journeys, but the only way you begin walking is by making the choice to take the steps. *(Written on 3/12/10)*

When Life Is Too Busy

I can't keep track of how many times I have heard people say "I'm so busy, I just can't find the time to get everything done." Their days are filled from early morning until late at night, trying to cram in some time to gulp down food, say hi to the family, and attempt the act of sleep. The kids are in all kinds of activities, or there are meetings to attend, or there are long days at the office. It's almost as if they need an assistant just to schedule their lives. Does any of this sound familiar?

If you notice any part of this being familiar, you may want to ask yourself why that is the case. If your life has become a runaway train on a track of endless things to get done, maybe it is time to stop, re-evaluate, and make changes in your life. Sometimes we have to make hard choices, and just because some activity or after school event looks fun and inviting, only so much is good for the body. Only so much can be done in a day and there are only 24 hours to a day, not 30!

Our bodies need rest and they need downtime, but if we constantly push them to the limits every day, we're overloading them for no good reason. The mentality of constantly pushing to get things done, adds a tremendous amount of stress to the body. Without giving ourselves a moment to relax or release all of this stress from deep within ourselves, we are traumatizing our lives daily.

Yes, you can keep this pace up for some time without major biological ramifications, but at some point, your body is going to say "I've had enough!" When it does that, you'll see all kinds of physical symptoms showing up from lack of sleep: tired and sore muscles, back pain, weight gain, high blood pressure and etc., etc., etc. You name it, the condition will show up. I realize that these conditions can be caused by many other things, but repetitive stress without release changes our biology.

For a long time in my life, I worked almost day and night. I had to be the best. I had to be perfect. I could not let anyone down. I had to be everything to everyone. It almost took me under. In fact, there wasn't much left of my life by the time I came to my senses. It took me some long, hard, and difficult moments to come back to reality and begin understanding what really did matter in life.

Our bodies have so much power and strength built into them and they can withstand a lot of pressure and stress, but all too often, we just keep pushing ourselves every day. We don't give ourselves the time we need to relax and let our minds rest, or to truly come down and experience a true state of peace within our lives. A day of vacation or a holiday here and there, isn't enough to do this. It should be a part of our daily and weekly lives.

So if this fits you, try to stop and evaluate all that you're doing in life. If you have to, take an inventory of how you spend your time and get a good grasp of what is going on. Are you giving yourself time to rest and relax each day, where your mind doesn't necessarily get input and stimulation, but is allowed to just clear out? Are you doing things that maybe are fun and inviting, but may just be too much and you need to slow down? Are you trying to be there for everyone and anyone associated with your life but you are absent with yourself? Maybe you've turned to stimulants such as coffee or food to get you up and going.

We all need balance in our lives and while too much stimulation can be harmful, too much sedation prevents us from really getting things done. If there is a balance between the two in our day, then we will most likely find more optimal performance for ourselves in life and accomplish much more. I still remember when I was working full time and going to massage school, my life was about as busy as it gets. However, on Saturday mornings I would go down and do Yoga. Even though it took about 2 hours out of my day, I found that I was able to accomplish much more during the rest of the weekend, and absorb more of my school work than if I didn't spend the time doing Yoga.

My hope is that everyone who reads this will give themselves the moments of rest and relaxation they deserve. This way, they can not only give themselves to all those around them in their life, but they can also give their own self what they truly need and desire. For if we don't take care of ourselves, who will? *(Written on 3/10/10)*

Chapter Six

Our Body Connections

While we live in and inhabit our
bodies, all too often, we are not as
connected to them as we need to be.
Let us be mindful of our bodies.

Selected Writings

The Essence Of Touch

Guided Relaxation Exercise

Relax!! Relax!!

Focus On Breathing, Part 1

Focus On Breathing, Part 2

Focus On Breathing, Part 3

The Essence Of Touch

When you hear the word massage, what thoughts come immediately to your mind? Is it thoughts of an intimate moment between you and a lover, or perhaps something you allowed yourself to indulge in while at a vacation resort, or on a tropical cruise? Maybe you are one of the fortunate people to have found how helpful massage is in your everyday life, getting rid of stress, centering yourself, and promoting a sense of well being.

Whatever your experience with massage, it has vast implications and benefits for our everyday life. Massage is more than intimate touch between people, and it is more than a momentary indulgence during a vacation or a tropical cruise. In some parts of the world, massage is an important way of life in maintaining one's health, and has been around since the beginning of time. Cultures from all parts of the world have practiced massage in one form or another to help heal, prevent illness, and bring a greater sense of what it means to live within our bodies.

Massage brings so many good things to our lives, including general overall stress reduction and physical relaxation. However, did you know that it also could help give you greater flexibility and improved posture, as well as better circulation? Massage also gives a calmer mind, which helps to improve thinking, along with the ability to monitor and respond to stress in a much more proactive way.

There are also the advantages of reduced anxiety in our lives, and an enhanced self-awareness that can bring so many new and exciting things into our lives. The list of benefits of massage is endless, as different people will experience different things from frequent massage.

The Touch Research Institute of Miami has studied the effects of massage at all stages of life, from infants to senior citizens. They found that massage, in addition to these previously mentioned benefits, also alters EEG readings in the direction of heightened awareness, improves immune function, and alleviates depressive symptoms. As you can see, massage isn't just a temporary indulgence; it is much more than that.

Often in our lives, we pay very little attention to our bodies, as far as what we need for ourselves. Even if we are aware of these things, the demands of daily life often preclude us from getting those things that we need. When there are the daily stresses of having to get the kids to school and their many events, or getting ourselves to work and to meetings, we often find very little time left to take care of ourselves in the way we should. Extending ourselves in too many directions, and not utilizing massage or relaxation like we should, is a recipe for disaster.

Of course each one of us promises and pledges that we will take care of ourselves, but often in life, it is not the case. If we can pledge to ourselves that we will take time out, once every two weeks or even once a month to get a massage, we will find that we can better prioritize and deal with our lives which will give us more energy and fulfillment, as we get the many tasks which are placed upon us accomplished. *(Written on 3/29/04)*

Guided Relaxation Exercise

Please take a moment to sit back, find a comfortable position, and relax. If you feel safe enough, close your eyes and focus on taking this time for yourself. These next few minutes are about you, and taking some time out of your busy day to relax. You are giving yourself this time. It is important for you to realize that right now you are in control. You can stop this at any time, and it is your right to do this.

So as we begin to take a few moments to rest and regenerate ourselves, begin to focus your mind on relaxing. Take a deep breath and then let it out. Take another deep breath and let it out. Notice how you feel before and after this. Now, take one more deep breath as you continue to focus on relaxing, and let it out. Just relax and remember that you are in control. Remember that by taking care of yourself, you are giving yourself the much needed strength and control that you deserve. Just relax.

As you begin to relax, focus on the muscles in your head and face. Notice the tightness in these muscles. Retract these muscles and let them expand to a more relaxed state. Again retract these muscles and then let them expand to a more relaxed state. Just relax, and remember you are safe and in control.

Now move your attention to your shoulder and neck muscles. Observe any tightness in these muscles. Retract these muscles and then let them expand to a more relaxed state. Notice how you feel before and after this. If you still feel tension in your shoulder and neck muscles, retract these muscles and then let them expand to a more relaxed state. Just relax into a more peaceful and quiet state of mind.

Focus your attention on your back, and take a few minutes to let the muscles of your back relax, pushing the stress and worries out of your body, for they are not needed right now. Just relax..... relax...... relax.

Now move your attention to your leg and feet muscles, as you relax. Push out all of the busyness of your mind and your life right now, as you continue to relax. Let these muscles relax and remember you are in control. Just relax now. Allow yourself to feel relaxed.

Take a couple of deep breaths as you continue to focus on relaxing. Your body so badly needs to relax and to enjoy the most that life has to offer. Relaxing will help reinvigorate your body to empower you and to give you the much needed strength for the day. Just continue to relax… relax…. relax… remembering that you are in control and you have a right to stop this at any time.

As you relax, find a quiet place in your mind, and join me as we journey to a different world. As you take off on this journey, you will notice beautiful mountains below you, filled with many wonderful colors, pretty sights, and fabulous smells. Off to one side, you will be able to see a lake, with a small and windy stream flowing down the rocks. Nestled among the lake and stream are very tall pine trees that provide much needed safety and solitude for you each day.

If you look close enough, you will be able to see the deer run and play as they invite you to share in the energy of the day. Above you, the sun is shining bright, as it gives you a blanket of warmth to let you know that you are a person who is able to be loved. Flying beside you are little white doves that help you to remember you are not alone. And as you are seeing all of these things, a warm gentle hand reaches down out of the sky to keep you safe, secure, and empower you for another day. Continue to gaze into the deep blue sky as you relax and regenerate your body.

As your body focuses on a greater sense of relaxation, allow your mind to remember this wonderful feeling. Remember that you deserve to allow yourself the time to relax and empower your life. Your body, muscles, and mind need this time to focus on the tasks of the day. You are in control, even though the worries and stress of the day may seem greater than your strength! Your strength is unlimited, and you are a person who has so much power and beauty.

I invite you as you are much more relaxed than you were, to take the renewed power of your life and embrace your accomplishments of the day. Take a moment now to take a deep breath and then let it out. As you do this, open your eyes now to an exciting new world. *(Written on 7/01/00)*

Relax!! Relax!!

I remember many times in massage school and various massage trainings, how the words "relax!" "relax!" were said to someone on the table in a very forceful, emphatic, and dramatic manner. It happened time and time again. While my specific example relates to massage, holding patterns in our bodies are experienced by virtually everyone, every day.

We all have them – even the most enlightened, most relaxed, calm person. It is part of the body. Many people, though, that I have worked on are not even aware of these holding patterns. In a moment, I'll tell you why that is.

Just imagine this example which I've seen hundreds of times. You're working on someone doing body work/massage and their arm is straight out – raised off the table. It is like a solid piece of wood with no flexibility, and may or may not be resting on the table. If this example is not quite clear, consciously take your arm for a moment and hold it out in front of you as rigidly as you can. Now you've got the image of what I'm talking about. And you would be amazed at just how many people are not even aware that they are doing this in the moment (I'd say 99.9% of them).

I come across examples of this all the time. Like I said, it is more normal than not to find this in a body, and most are not even aware of it. It doesn't have to be the arm either. It could be a neck, shoulder, back, leg, hip, or just about any part of the body. Other areas where this is common are the legs and hip. While it may not appear rigid like my example of the arm, you can notice it in how people walk (their gait), how they stand, sit, and get around. I see it all the time.

By now I hope you have the point I'm trying to make. I'm sure it is hard for most people reading this to really understand, and while it may seem obvious to take note of, it is often hidden from direct sight of the person experiencing it. I've seen people look right at what I was describing above, and not even note that their arm or other body part is as rigid as it is.

So why does this happen? It comes down to the disconnect between the mind and body. We live in a world where we are often split into two parts, these two parts being the mind and the body. Although we know deep down there is a connection, the communication between the two is often blurred, severed, or rerouted. Do you ever find yourself trying to make a tough decision, and you make the statement "I make decisions with my gut instinct"? Or maybe it is when you might say "I have a feeling in my bones." This doesn't necessarily mean that a person is consciously connecting their mind and their body, but they sure are doing it unconsciously.

So too, when people have the disconnect in their bodies, they may very likely resemble the examples I gave above. The mind does not even connect to how rigid the body may be, and yet one can't function without the other. It is as if instead of having one whole part, you have two divided parts.

Now here's where I tell you that you're off the hook though. I mean, after all, you can't control these things consciously for the most part. Right? Or can you? So maybe you're not off the hook then. While you can make a conscious choice to become aware of these things, they don't reside in the conscious part of your brain. And all at once, everyone says "hold on a minute, you just contradicted yourself."

Okay let's explain this a little further. Body holding patterns that everyone has come from all sorts of events, sources, past times, stress, trauma – you name it, it probably had an influence on it. The influences may come from things that you really wouldn't suspect, as well. So we know they exist. The thing is, they exist within the subconscious part of our brain, or the unconscious mind. They are a bunch of neural pathways that have been forged and are on automatic pilot. They don't require you to do anything to show up; they just appear. They don't require you to think "I'm going to hold my arm like this," as in the earlier example; the neural pathways just do this.

So when people constantly tell someone "relax!," or "just let go," or "don't worry about that," or insert your common phrase here, they are usually barking up the wrong tree. You're trying to communicate with a part of a person that can't communicate with you, because the communication line has not been created and established yet. You could repeat your common phrases all day long to someone, and they would most likely bounce off of them like light reflecting off a mirror. That's the subconscious or unconscious part of ourselves in play.

By this point, you may be thinking, "Well, if I can't control it, then I'm doomed forever with this part, because if I can't access it and I can't communicate with it, there's not much I can do." The only thing is there is something you can do. You can consciously make a choice to connect with it, but in so doing, you need to strip away all judgment, all attachment to it, all fear, and just be there with that part of yourself in the most loving, free of fear, full of courage way. That's not easy, of course, but it can be done. Having someone there with you that cleaned out their own closets already, and can stand in that place with you with true love, free of fear and full of courage, will be an eye opening experience. Some people call this "holding the space open," and that would be an accurate portrayal of the concept I'm trying to point out.

The whole point of this is we have parts of our self that are buried deep within us. They reside in a place of unconsciousness, and if we try to communicate with them in a conscious way, the language will be misunderstood and not heard. If we acknowledge that they exist and meet it with love, courage, and total acceptance, we'll find we will speak the same language and be understood.

And while this applies to body work, it also applies to our communication between ourselves and others each day.

How many times do you suggest to someone that they just move on and forget about what happened? They just need to let it go. They just need to forgive. While these all may be noble and worthy things to say, they are often being communicated to the part of the person that is still unconscious, as the events are still locked within the subconscious mind.

If the person is not able to access these deep caves within their subconscious mind and body, then it will be very hard for them to hear and understand what you're trying to convey to them. Instead, try being there with them and listening, and just helping hold the space open. You may be surprised at just how that helps the person more. Often times by doing nothing, you are doing more for the person. By doing nothing, I mean you are getting your own life's stuff out of the way, so you can just be there with the person without judgment or anticipation or expectation.

And believe me, most people don't really want to be burdened with all of these holding patterns or holding events in their lives. They really do want to flee from them. The problem is they do not know how to let go, and often the fears associated with these patterns are greater in their eyes than the rewards of freedom that result. *(Written on 11/01/08)*

Focus On Breathing, Part 1

How often do you stop throughout your day and focus on your breathing? Is it shallow and rapid, slow and deep, or is it hardly existent? Can you even tell that you are breathing, or sense the qualities of it?

Yet breathing is what gives us our life and our energy in a day. Without it and without the oxygen it provides, we would not be in a good state of being. So, why is it that we fail to pay attention to something that is so vital to our existence?

Most likely we are so busy and hurried in our days that stopping to pause for a moment is not on our calendar. Stopping to check in with ourselves to see how we are breathing is not something we most likely feel we have the time to do. This is sad, because it only takes a minute. Our awareness of what is going on with this vital process can give us so much more fulfillment in our lives, and replenish our bodies in ways that we may not think about.

Sometimes what may be the most obvious, simple things in life, end up being so difficult. We are much more concerned about getting to the next meeting, completing a task that the boss is hammering us on, or competing for a deadline. While those are all noble and worthy tasks for our day, if we fail to take a moment and check in with our bodies, especially in regards to breathing, we may just be forcing ourselves through our day with more difficulty than is needed.

Consider for a moment that if you check in with your breathing, you might realize that you're operating out of stress and from a frantic pace. But if you're able to slow yourself down for a moment, just think of what that would do to help you accomplish all that you need. One moment of checking in with your breathing may help you make corrective changes that will empower and give you a boost into what needs to be accomplished. Otherwise, it is like adding water to your gasoline tank. While it may keep the engine running at a minimum, it won't get you as far as the ultimate fuel source.

Checking in with your breathing isn't as hard as you may think it is, and it isn't as time-consuming as you might think either. There are some simple things you can do during your day at just about any moment, and if you do them, you'll be much better off in the long run. You'll be more productive, more centered and much more full of life.

Read part 2 (following section) for more on this topic, "Focus On Breathing - 30 Second Exercise", where we discuss a quick way of checking in with your breathing that you can do at almost any time and in almost any place. *(Written on 6/09/10)*

Focus On Breathing, Part 2

As you can see from the previous article "Focus On Our Breathing", stopping to check out breathing in our day is very important. While it may seem that this is something you neither have the time to do, nor the place, I am here to tell you that you can do this at any time or in almost any place. It is simple, and yet it can be profound for our day.

You probably do not want to do this if you are in a car, or in a situation that requires your constant alertness and awareness of what is going on. Please use your judgment in what place is appropriate, and what places are not appropriate. Sitting at your desk or in a break room, or even outside on a park bench would all be great places for this scenario. Even standing in a line waiting for an event, or at a checkout in a store would work as well. There are many places and many different moments that you can do this. Your willingness and imagination are the keys to finding them.

So now that you've found the appropriate place and time, let's get started.

Try to find a comfortable way to sit or stand, so that you're body is in as relaxed a position as it can be. Let your arms rest comfortably by your side, or in a position where you can just let the tension go. Drop your shoulders a little, and just recognize any tension that is there. Feel throughout your body for a moment, and just recognize any tension that may be present and that you can sense. Give yourself a moment where you just focus on your body letting go, and feeling it sink down into the floor or chair or wherever you may be.

Now as you do that, take a moment and only focus on your breathing. For the next 30 seconds, you want to do nothing else but focus on breathing. No thoughts or tasks or appointments that you need to get done are needed. This next 30 seconds are just for you, and you can give yourself permission to let those things wait patiently away from you.

Take a moment and close your eyes. Begin by feeling your breath as you inhale, and notice the depth of your inhale. Feel the exhale and how far the air is released through your body. You're not trying to influence anything at this point, just observing and acknowledging what is going on, without any judgment. Just continue to focus on this and be with your breathing, honoring it and respecting all that is there. This is your life blood and what keeps you going through your day. It is there for you, to support you, and give you all that you need for your life. Just continue to observe your inhale, and your exhale. Feel what it is like for your body to inhale and exhale and what your breathing is like when you notice this.

After about 30 seconds, begin to open your eyes and note the depth of your breath, the pace of it, and all that you could feel. Did it change as you continued to observe it? Did it slow down and become deeper? If not, don't worry, but just observe and note what took place. The more you do this, the more connected you will become to your breathing. You'll be able to monitor it much easier as you do this more, and you will become more aware of it throughout your day.

Take note of how you feel after this. Do you feel more centered and more focused? Maybe you just feel a sense of peace and rest or relaxation. What about tension in your body? Do your shoulders or neck or back feel a little less tense? You may or may not be able to notice these things but if you do, take note of them.

Hopefully after 30 seconds of focusing on your breath and your body, you will be much more aligned with your day, and ready to focus on what lies ahead. If you did this little 30-second-to-one minute exercise each day, or even twice a day, your day would go so much differently. My challenge to you is to try this and see what happens, and then try it for a month. Find out what is possible from doing something as simple as this exercise of focusing on your breathing. I have a feeling that it will greatly impact your life in ways that you didn't even realize were possible.

Read on to the next section (Part 3), for more about the importance of noticing our breath and checking in with this part of our body. *(Written on 6/10/10)*

Focus On Breathing, Part 3

If you have read the past two sections "Focus On Our Breathing" and "Focus On Our Breathing - 30 Second Exercise", then you already have understood why focusing on breathing is important, and learned a quick way that you can do this.

Breathing is so powerful, and I'm sure each person reading this is aware of that. However, we often forget, and neglect the most basic thing we do outside of pumping blood through our veins. All too often, we go through life just assuming we are breathing as we need to, but we never stop to check to see how we are actually breathing.

I remember sitting through many counseling or bodywork sessions, and having people remind me to breathe. At first I was startled by their comments for me to remember to breathe, because I thought I was. However, as I have since found out, there are times that I almost hold my breath or I just don't breathe! It may sound strange, but I have witnessed this in not only myself, but in many others.

As a massage therapist, I have used breath work to help people really go in and release deep, long held pain within their bodies in a very short time. Having people use their breath in a very directed way, as I work on them, is powerful and makes my job much easier and their results more profound. It is important to note that each one of us can go deep within our own bodies, using our breath, to release tension, pain, and long held somatic memories.

Here are some thoughts about how you might actually go about working with breath on your own. These are additional methods to the 30 second exercise I shared in the previous section. They build upon the previous exercises.

1) Find a comfortable place such as a bed, massage table, or maybe a lounge chair on your patio. Get yourself comfortable and make sure the place you are

lying on has much support, but is also soft and gentle on your body. You could also sit up in a meditative style if you want, but I find that the body really lets go when it is not trying to hold itself up. It doesn't make sense to me to sit up, having tension in my body while trying to let go of that tension. Maybe it makes sense to some, but not to me in my experiences.

2) If you have a pulse meter, check your pulse before you begin and establish a baseline of where you are. This helps greatly because then you will truly know what is going on within your body, and you will see through measurement what effect it will have had upon you. There will be no second guessing, or having your mind trick you into thinking that something happened. There is too much of that in our society and in our healing world, where people think something happened, when in all reality, very little if anything did.

I use the Finger Pulse Oximeter OctiveTech 300Pro. The reason I use this pulse meter is that it tells me in real time what my pulse is, and how the wave forms of my pulse appear. It gives me some very good and helpful information. Plus, it shows me exactly what is going on, not what my mind may be tricking me into believing is going on.

3) To begin, just get comfortable in the place you have chosen, and lie there for a few minutes doing nothing but just sensing what it is like to lie on the table. I'm going to use the word "table", referring to a massage table, to make this easier to explain. What does it feel like to lie there on the table? Are you completely comfortable, or can you add a pillow or change your position to feel more comfortable? Just sense all of that and take it in for a few minutes. Focus on allowing all your busy thoughts and things that you need to accomplish to stand outside the door of the room you

are in. You can always pick them up at the door later if you so choose, but for now, they are not needed.

4) As you begin to feel the comfort and support of the table, begin to focus in on your breathing. Notice the inhale and exhale, the rise and fall of your breath. This is not the time for judgment, just observation: observation which allows you to look at it through caring, loving, and accepting eyes. Take note of the depth or shallowness of your breath, as well as the speed of it. What is it like? How deep is it, or how shallow is it? Maybe trying to sense this is difficult at best for you and if it is, take note of that. Consider giving yourself the option of just allowing that feeling to be there and to be okay with it, not expecting anything more than is happening.

5) Continue breathing, and then see if there is any change in how shallow or deep it is, how slow or fast it is, and any other qualities you may find. Keep noticing this and focusing upon your breath. While you are doing this, you may begin to notice things within your body. This could range from minor shaking and trembling, to maybe a body part moving on its own. You might also notice an itching sensation or tingling, as well as you might notice areas where it is almost a numb feeling. Emotions such as crying and laughter, among other things, may be showing up. There may be unexplained pains, or stiffness that is present. You may see colors or feel all kinds of sensations within your body. Accept and honor all these things, for they are your messages and your gifts to bringing about greater awareness within your body.

6) Keep your focus on what is happening within your body and with your breath. While all the experiences may be exciting, and it could be easy to get lost in

those, keep your focus on what you can sense and feel within your body. For this is where the true healing will take place, and lead you to a greater awareness. If you begin to find areas of discomfort and pain, or strong emotions coming up, begin to shift your breathing to these areas and imagine filling yourself up with the power of your breath. You may notice that your breathing speeds up as if you were running a race, and that is perfectly okay. Allow your breathing to go where it needs to, and then keep observing to see how things change in your body. Are areas less tense, less painful? Have emotions that maybe you were feeling and experiencing changed? Maybe some of the things you noticed have shifted from one area to another. Maybe you're feeling heat rise from your body. Welcome all these things and just continue to observe everything that is taking place. Continue to allow yourself to be with what is happening, and just allow it to take place without trying to control, change, manipulate, or judge it.

7) As your body moves through the feelings and as you begin to feel and sense more of your breathing, allow your body to sink down into the table and find a moment of peace and rest. Know that you do not have to solve everything in your life that may be showing up in your body at one time. Sometimes, short bursts of doing this type of exercise is healing far beyond comprehension. So just allow your body to come back down to a moment of stillness and rest on the table, giving it honor and thanking it for being there for you.

8) After lying there for a few minutes, you might check your pulse again with the pulse meter we discussed. How did your pulse change? Is it significantly lower? Is the wave form more pointed and even? Then match that up with how you feel now versus how you felt

before you started. What changed in your body? What changed in your mind?

Honor all these things and take them all in. Treasure them as gifts of awareness, for the more you do exercises like this, the more they will connect together and yield so much to your life. For you have the power to do so much within your own body. Yes, there may be some difficult challenges, in which you want a safe and supportive person there with you to help coach you through them. We are all much more powerful than we realize, and we can do so much on our own that will give us so much in our lives.

If you have found this helpful and you're working with it, I would love to hear your experiences. For I know in my own life, some of the basic things that I just described have helped me push through so much, and helped me heal in my own awareness. My hope is that as a result of this exercise that your life will grow in a more rich awareness and it will help you further your own journey of self discovery and healing. *(Written on 6/11/10)*

Chapter Seven

In The Moment

The greatest moment we have in our lives is the moment we are experiencing. Anything in the past is already gone, and the future has not yet arrived.

Selected Writings

Walking The Labyrinth

Mindfully Present

Mistakes In Life

Cats Live In The Moment

Mindless Humans

Are You Mindful And Creative?

Walking The Labyrinth

To learn more about what a labyrinth is, please see my blog posts at mindbodythoughts.blogspot.com, "What Is A Labyrinth", by Trish Kalhagen (4/27/10). This particular account is of my first time walking a labyrinth. It was an experience that I will cherish forever.

Today, I walked the labyrinth for the first time.

"I don't know what they are doing but it looks nice," said one lady.

"It looks like a nice maze or something," said another lady.

Of course, these were the words I heard as I walked a portion of the labyrinth today at the M.D. Anderson Cancer Center in Orlando, Florida. There was a group of ladies that came out to stand on the terrace, not knowing that we were walking a labyrinth as a spiritual healing practice. They did not realize what this was about, and so I heard what they said, but just patiently focused my mind and continued my walk.

After all, it was not that long ago that I would have probably said the same things, and thought this was just a fancy maze. I had no idea it was rooted in spirituality (note that I did not say religion), and is part of one's own personal journey into reflection on life, releasing things not desired, and integrating your life with what you receive. Even though I remembered posting a blog entry on April 27, 2010, titled Labyrinth Experience (see the blog at mindbodythoughts.blogspot.com), I did NOT remember that these were the parts of a labyrinth experience – the releasing, receiving, and integrating. So now, any doubts I had about the experience have just been reduced to zero! I'll explain more about this, as I write about my own labyrinth journey today.

I was the first to start walking and to be honest, I was a little nervous. I really wasn't sure what I was supposed to do, other than walk slowly and stay open. My fear of maybe getting off the path and getting mixed up weighed in, as well as people most likely watching me from the windows of the building that surrounded us. Of course, my friends were there, and I was a little self conscious about them observing me, in case I might have been doing anything wrong.

So planting my feet firmly at the start of the path into the labyrinth, I just stopped and focused my mind, breathing in to my body and just feeling my body as it was grounded to the stones below my feet. I knew that it was all about putting one foot in front of the other, and just following the path laid out before me. As I took one step after another, my legs felt so wobbly that I could barely walk, let alone stand up.

I began to get fearful that I would not be able to walk, which of course triggered many fears within me. In my mind, I began to rationalize that walking like this should be no different than walking in any other way during my day. Yet, I was really struggling to get my feet steady on the ground. It felt as if hurricane force winds were blowing me from side to side, yet the wind was gently blowing that day.

Finally, I just stopped and took some deep breaths, trying to honor and respect my body and just connect with my legs. It felt good to stop and just take in what I was feeling. Whatever it was, I knew it was very strong. Soon I was walking again, but as I did my feet became wobbly and I struggled to get my feet on the ground. Why was I having such a difficulty in walking, I pondered? I didn't have an answer to that, but I soon realized that I would just need to go slower and allow myself to be there with my wobbly legs, uncertainty, and all my fears.

My breathing was somewhat difficult as well, and I kept stopping along the path before me to just focus on my breath and keeping my feet planted firmly on the ground. At some point, I began to notice that walking became much easier, that my feet were much more firm than they had been. Yet, I was puzzled in my mind as to what changed.

It was all the same material and all the same stones. The patterns changed in length, but were all basically the same. I could not come up with an answer, but knew that something had shifted. As I began to notice this, I realized that my breathing was becoming much easier. Up until this point, I felt as if a heavy weight was bearing down on my chest and diaphragm, making it truly difficult to breathe.

I kept my eyes on the path ahead of me and kept walking. I felt the ease of the moment increase, which brought joy to my body. Then, all at once, I felt as if the sun was beaming down upon me and just as if I was getting a lot of information, from some source. It was almost like a computer download. I could not make out the specific information but I could feel it as energy waves coming into me. It was a strange sensation that I felt, but in many ways, there was a familiarity to it.

As I continued to feel all of these, I noticed with each step I took, it was easier and my walking was freer. I was not as concerned about where I was on the path or how I would stay on it. It just felt natural to continue walking. It was a feeling of freedom, of ease, and everything coming together.

The more I walked, the more I felt almost like a child wanting to skip along. It was as if I could hear children laughing and giggling although none were present. It was as if I felt like a happy-go-lucky person with no cares or concerns in the world. It was a good feeling. It was a welcomed feeling.

Continuing along the path, my attention began to turn toward the building I was surrounded by, and the people in it who were undoubtedly dealing with some of the most difficult forms of fear that they would ever deal with, which was cancer. While I personally don't know what that is to deal with, I've had enough experiences in my life to understand so much about fear.

Automatically, as if following some unknown script, my prayers began turning to thinking of these people. I began to ask for strength for those that faced these things, and for support for them during these times, as well as their loved ones, the doctors, and caregivers. As we were walking out to the labyrinth on the terrace of the building, a patient was walking out the door with a caregiver, and exclaimed "Oh it feels so good to see the outside." My heart heard that, and connected with some of my old fears of the past, as I was moved to tears. For this person and the others, I offered the prayer of support and love and healing to them. I was a guest in their building.

My next prayer drifted to the thoughts of the meditation prayer Dr. Masaru Emoto had asked the world to contemplate. It was the prayer for the Gulf Of Mexico and the oil spill. I offered my own version up to the labyrinth and the universe, asking that the reefs be protected and the oil be contained before it did any more damage.

As I continued to walk, my prayers turned toward all those around me in the world. It was a collective group of people that I focused on, asking that they open their eyes and become aware of more than they currently see. I long for people to wake up and connect with a part of life and the universe that they now treat as a stranger. Hearts close, and anger rules while the bodies and minds are at two opposite worlds. I cry for the hurt and pain inflicted upon humanity. I weep for the people who struggle to see with eyes that are closed. I weep for the hatred and fear that has infected the lives of many. My prayer is for all the people of this world who are still trying to find their way along their own paths.

The next prayer then turned toward myself, knowing that I have been struggling through some intense times of wondering what's next for me. Where do I go? How do I get there? Filled lately with so many questions, and not allowing myself the time to ponder the answers that most likely lie before me, I want to know, where do I go? What steps must I take?

As I began to ponder that prayer, my attention turned toward the labyrinth. Here I had entered the beginning point, not really knowing how the path would get me all the way back to the starting point. If I looked at it carefully, the labyrinth seemed very confusing, and yet, it had a particular flow and shape to it. You really didn't have to worry about where to go, because if you just followed the path and put one foot in front of the other, you found yourself moving through the patterns. It wasn't a difficult thing to do, but yet, if I had stopped to worry too much about how to get through this maze of geometric shapes, I would have never taken a step.

Yet, all of it unfolded as I journeyed on. I really didn't have to think about it. It just unfolded as I moved forward. It happened as I needed it to happen, and if it was coming too fast, I could slow down. If I wanted to go faster, I would just pick up the pace. It was a path. It was a journey. All I needed was right in front of me the entire time.

Much like my life. As I look back on the path that I've already walked, I can see how it is connected. At the time, I could not see that, but then if I just continue to walk the path, I will be on my journey. I need not worry about what is coming up in the next section, or how I will get around the next bend.

All I need to do is put one of my feet in front of the other and keep following the path. That's it. That's all I need. The rest will be waiting on the path as I approach it. It will not come a moment too soon, nor will I walk by it for it is all on my path. It is all part of me to hold, honor, and cherish. It is there to sustain me, give me direction, and help me on to the next bend, twist, or turn in my path. How hard is that? How easy is that, I ponder to myself?

As my thoughts grew to a close, I noticed that I was coming upon the beginning point. It was where I had started this particular part of my journey, and where this part of my journey came to a close. What comes next is as unknown as walking on the labyrinth path. Does it matter? Most likely not! For if I get worried and concerned about having to know all what lies ahead, what do I profit? I'm just robbing myself, through the useless energy of trying to control something which is not ready to unfold, or appear to my consciousness.

Instead, if I use that energy to welcome all that I've been given and all that I've learned, realized, and grown through, then there is the possibility that I am taking giant leaps on my path, rather than small baby steps. So much I'm realizing that the "now" is the most important thing I have. It is more precious than gold. It is all I have. The next minute, the next project, the next income source is beyond my grasp. It is in a moment we do not have and cannot obtain. In much the same way, if I focus upon the moments gone by, then I am taking away from the joys of my current moments. It is best if I can remember to live with the "now", because it is what I have and it is what is the most important for me.

This was my first time walking the labyrinth and I'll be forever grateful for the experience, the wisdom, and the courage that I had to do this. It was a very spiritual experience with friends that helped me to see what lies before my eyes. I'm honored to have walked this labyrinth. After I began to write about this experience, I realized that I had gone through the stages of releasing, receiving, and integrating, without being aware that these were the stages I would experience. What a wonderful gift to realize just how this was manifested, when I was not consciously aware that it would happen in this way. I am forever humbled by this experience. *(Written on 6/21/10)*

Mindfully Present

Have you ever just stopped and listened to what is around you? Have you noticed all the sounds that may be present? Sure, there are times when we hear the familiar sounds we know very well. But, just how much do we really hear and notice and take in? So often we are too busy in our lives to notice and be mindful of our surroundings.

If you really want to reset and be mindfully present, try quieting yourself and listening to what is around you. You may want to take a notebook with you and record all that you hear. See how many different sounds you can pick up. Observe all that you can see. Notice everything that is going on. Allow yourself to be part of the moment, pushing aside all other thoughts, worries, and things you need to accomplish for your day. This time is about allowing yourself to be mindfully present in the moment.

There is no better moment of rest that is as energizing, refreshing, and inviting as surrounding yourself with the symphony of nature. All too often, we are too busy in our lives to just stop and let our mind, body, and spirit be in the moment.

It is so easy for us to get caught up in our days, filled with electronics of all flavors, types and sizes. We are constantly bombarded by noise from the TV news, the cars rushing by, or the chatter of our fellow humans. While many of these things may be a necessary part of our day, we need to balance our lives with time away from these noises. We cannot expect to let go when we are constantly bombarded with noise that never stops.

So find a place in nature somewhere, as far removed from the city hustle and bustle that you can. Take some fresh, cool water with you. When you arrive at your spot, make yourself comfortable. If you're having a difficult time quieting your thoughts, acknowledge them and then just sit there focusing on your breathing. Tell yourself, if you need to, that all the stresses and worries of your day are not needed in this moment. Let them go for now, because they will be there when you are done, although they may appear different.

Then as you sink into the moment, just allow yourself to be there as an observer. Take note of all that you see, feel, sense, observe, and pick up. If it feels right, try to record these things in a notebook, but stay mindful and present. Just sit there with all that is going on. Take in everything and see what shows up that you may not easily see. Just observe and notice it all.

Once you have finished, be thankful for this time. Then, notice how the rest of your day goes. Is there a change in how you view things in your life? Is there a change or shift in you? Do you feel a sense of ease? Just observe and notice all of it. Take it all in. *(Written on 7/11/10)*

Mistakes In Life

Mistakes are something that I've always been pretty hard on myself for, throughout my entire life. There are plenty of reasons, as I'm sure many others out there would attest to as well. I could delve into the details of all of these, but it most likely would not further this particular discussion. Of course, it is important to note that I am not saying you should not travel into these areas of your life. On the contrary, I feel it is important to go in and reclaim these misfires of communication in your mind that distort mistakes. Once you do, you offer your brain a different path to travel when these circumstances come up.

I am very creative, but as I create, I get very critical of myself. This is especially true when it comes to creating music. Most of the music I play is songs that I create in the moment. They are not repeated from anyone or anything, but are totally what happens at the moment my hands rest on the keyboard. If you had the opportunity to be around me when I am creating, you would more than likely hear me say at some point as I was listening to a playback of the song, "there was a mistake." The average person or even the talented musician would not hear the mistake. That is because when I hear it played back, it seems like a mistake, since it is not the way I heard the music come together in my mind. And yet, I am realizing now that those little moments that I call mistakes, have led to some wonderful moments in the songs I have created. It has given them a depth and dimension of their own, and without these "mistakes", they would not be all that they are.

One of my favorite authors, Ellen Langer, in the book *On Becoming An Artist*, writes about mistakes on page 81. Paraphrasing this page, she talks about how mistakes make us up as individuals. Without them, we would not show all that we are, and we most likely would miss new places. Our mistakes help us to be unique and interesting rather than dull and predictable.

So if we feel we really have to embrace the fear that we make mistakes in life, why not try turning the tables on the thought process for a moment. If we see mistakes as an opportunity toward greater awareness or insight, then the person who makes many mistakes has many opportunities in life. Just imagine having all those opportunities.

Of course if we take the mindful approach to what we consider mistakes, then all that you are and all the potential you have has the opportunity to shine as bright as the brightest star. *(Written on 10/04/09)*

Cats Live In The Moment

Have you ever noticed how a cat lives in the moment? They don't necessarily worry about where they are going to find food tomorrow or the next day, or what activities they will do. There are no long term planned out goals, and no events they have to attend. There aren't any to do lists and deadlines. They just live in the moment.

While maybe we as humans cannot live our lives completely as a cat does, there are many things we can do to live in the moment. Often as humans, we put so many demands upon ourselves, and we create more work and stress for ourselves than is needed. Consider for a moment everything you do in a day. What is the purpose of it? Is it all necessary? Yes, there is the shopping, the taking care of a family, performing your career duties, and interacting with friends. That is all true.

However, again I ask, is it all necessary? And if it is, could there be another way to do things? What about a way with more ease, simplicity, and focus? What if you stopped for a moment and considered all you had to do, letting the full breadth of your creativity and analytical abilities ponder what was before you? Perhaps, this would be a better way to make it through your day.

We often react to situations as they come at us, and in those moments, the stress and tension is higher than if we were in a relaxed state. What if we just paused for a moment and looked at the situation? Where might that get us? I would suggest that the outcome of taking a pause in the moment would get us further than just reacting to what was going on, and trying to solve the situation immediately. Sure, there are times when time is of the essence, and so as we think about this, let us keep that in perspective.

As I go back to watching a cat, I see just how they live in the moment. When they feel like eating, they eat. When they want to play, they play. When they want to sleep, they sleep. It is purely in the moment. They are, for the most part, tuned into what their body needs. While we as humans cannot live like cats do, we can take pauses in our own lives and focus on living in the moment every chance we get. We could experience life from living in the moment if we allowed ourselves to do this.

Living in the moment can come in all forms no matter how busy you are in a day. There can be the step outside the office door for two minutes, to take a deep breath of fresh air and allow yourself to feel it as it fills every cell of your body. There can be the 30 seconds sitting at your desk, just allowing yourself to focus on your breathing and feeling how all of it fills every sense of your being. Maybe a stand up and stretch during your day in a busy office can allow you to connect with that body you live in all 24 hours of the day. Of course these are just examples in a busy day for you to stop, pause, and enjoy a moment of living.

For me, I try to mix in my day many different ways of pausing. The many possibilities will be different from person to person. I can be at home with myself as I'm working in a garden, feeling every grain of soil as I connect with the earth, which to me is a source of strength and grounding. As the sun warms my body, I can feel revived again throughout every functioning cell of my body. It may be just a stroll down the street in the evening air, or a ride through the country. It might be stopping and listening to, or observing the birds flying around me, or seeing the ripples through the trees and lake of my favorite local park.

Sometimes it is sitting by the window with my cat in my arms, observing the wind moving the trees through the air without effort. It could even be a simple moment listening to some beautiful music that takes my mind away from the busy moments in my day. There are so many examples that I could give, and I'm sure in your own life, you will be able to find those simple things. Treat it as a treasure hunt and see all of the great gifts we have waiting just waiting, for us to accept them.

I remember when I was going to massage school at Educating Hands and working full time. School was three nights a week, plus often one of the weekend days, and work was at least eight hours a day. Between school and studying, along with daily life activities, there was not much time left for anything else. One of the things I did was to take yoga on Saturday mornings. Sure, it took a couple of hours or so by the time I traveled there and took the yoga class. Often I would wonder if I was making good use of my time, until the class was over and I would see the benefits.

Yoga would give me a time of just stopping, clearing my mind, and connecting with my body. The rest of the day, I would be much more productive than I would have been if I had not gone to yoga. Just stopping and taking a pause offers us so much. Indeed it offers us life!

I hope you will join me in finding pauses and moments of stillness in our days. Whether it is something elaborate, or something very simple, may we all find a way to stop, clear our minds, and just connect to the bodies we inhabit 24 hours a day. For if we all do this, we will have given our days, our bodies, and our lives so much life! *(Written on 7/19/10)*

Mindless Humans

Often in our day, we have so many influences that determine the course of our actions, our thoughts, our consciousness, and in general just how we view our day. Yet we fail to see the totality of these individual events as they dramatically impact our lives. We often see them as unconnected events, without any significance to the higher purpose of our self or of the universe as a whole.

What events am I referring to? These events are the moments in our every day existence that we barely notice, yet account for the many tasks we do. They are things we have to do in order to take care of ourselves or family members in any given day. It may be a job that we go to, running our kids to daycare or after school events, or dealing with a myriad of mundane tasks. Yes, all these tasks are important and critical to our lives, for if we stopped doing them, there would be serious repercussions for us. Even watching TV shows and news, while appearing to inform or entertain you, may actually result in you being disconnected and not conscious or mindful.

These mundane tasks are important, but there is a point to all this. When was the last time you walked out the door in the morning, and just listened to the birds sing with joy? When was the last time you went to lunch and stopped to pause for a moment to feel the sun hitting your face, giving you a warmth and energy that felt so invigorating? When was the last time, while taking your child to daycare or an activity, that you truly listened to what they were saying and not just thinking about all the things you needed to get done? When was the last time, you just stopped for a moment and noticed your breathing and your body, and just how good it felt to do that?

We all have our mundane tasks in our mundane lives that we have to do. That is a fact of life, unless you are a lottery winner and can pick and choose everything you do in life.

However, even people who are wealthy have mundane tasks that they must do. All of us have to get out of bed at some point during the day and eat, groom ourselves, and do whatever it is that we feel is important. No matter how fortunate or wealthy we are, these things are a given for our day. Since we can't escape these normal tasks, can we not enjoy them in a mindful way?

As stated by Ellen Langer in her book, *On Becoming an Artist: Reinventing Yourself Through Mindful Creativity* (page 11), we have become mindless without really acknowledging or questioning that we have. This is a powerful statement, and is what I'm referring to as I talk about being mindless during our mundane tasks that we do each day. We all do it, no matter who we are or how advanced we are. Some people are better than others at bringing mindfulness into their days instead of just being mindless.

So what can we do? One of the things that each of us can do is just taking a moment out of our day, and being with ourselves in the moment.

We can do this by spending a few moments (30 seconds would be enough for this exercise) and noticing our breath. Feeling the rise and fall of our breath, how shallow or deep it is, and even how rapid or slow it is will connect us to our breath. By connecting to our breath, we will connect our mind with our body. If you stay with this exercise for a few moments, you'll begin to feel the effects of it on your body in how centered you feel, how at home you feel, and even the tension within yourself. You need not pay anyone for an experience like this, because you can do it with yourself at any time of the day or night. It is simple but effective.

In his book discussions with Oprah Winfrey on *A New Earth: Awakening to Your Life's Purpose* (Oprah's Book Club, Selection 61), Eckhart Tolle did a very powerful example of this. He had everyone sit there for 30 seconds, wherever they were, and focus on their breath. It was an amazing experience for many, and once again I saw the power of something that was this simple.

Another simple thing we can do is when we are walking out the door in the morning, just stop and listen to all that we can hear. Some of you may find many noises such as cars and city sounds, but see if you can listen beyond that. How many different birds do you hear singing? How fast are the chirps coming from the birds? Is the wind rustling through the leaves of the trees, and how does that sound? You may hear a dog barking in the background, or a cat meowing. What other sounds do you pick up?

If sounds do not work for you, try picking up on the colors you see as you walk out of your house. Can you notice the different colors of the landscape around your house, or your neighbor's? What if you look at the trees and see all the colors on the tree? How many different colors are there, and how many different shades of the color green can you see? I'm only scratching the surface with all that you can see, because the same things can be applied if you just look at the sky and clouds.

There are many ways you can be mindful in your day, including feeling the warmth of the sun as you step out of a building, or staring at the clouds and creating cloud images in your mind. You could even take a moment when you're in the shower, and feel the sensation of the hot or cold water on your skin. Give yourself plenty of time to eat so that you can actually taste and enjoy your food, without having your daily tasks flooding your conscious mind. These are a few examples, and if you practice being mindful instead of mindless, you'll find many more.

Please don't think this is all there is to mindfulness. It is much more than that. Try to take all that you pick up in these exercises and see how it makes you feel within your body. Do you get a warm glow or tingle? Do you feel goose bumps on your skin? Do you feel your body sink down into a state of relaxation? Do you sense your breath slowing down and becoming fuller?

There are so many ways that we can be impacted by becoming mindful. When you feel it in your body, you have truly crossed over from being a mindless human to being mindful of your life, your day, and your moments. At this point, life will be much more rewarding and abundant for you, while becoming more conscious. *(Written on 12/01/09)*

Are You Mindful And Creative?

At one time in my life, being creative, in my mind, meant being a painter, a writer, or a musician, among other things. Creative, to me, meant something you did in your spare time that was only for these things. Outside of that, I always figured that creativity really had little place in my everyday life. Sure, many of the companies I have worked for gave lip service to thinking outside the box, but few nurtured the concepts past an evaluation period or company meeting.

For most of my life, I did not think I was that creative. It was not something that was allowed to be in existence while I was a kid growing up, except for when I put together model semi trucks or various crafts my mom would buy me for Christmas. It was always about finding a job and making a decent income, and functioning in life like our society requires. There was no time for creative moments unless you did them on your own time, and there was no support for this.

Yes, I was able to practice and learn the piano as a kid, but whenever I tried to be creative and just play from my center of creativity like I do today, it was often met with criticism by those who could not even play one note. I still remember the time I was creating in the moment with some music, and while it wasn't a polished piece of music at that moment, my father made sure he told me that I made many mistakes. This was not helpful, and it led me to hide my creative in-the-moment ability, if anyone was within hearing range.

Following the rules of society, I went to college and pursued a degree in a field of study I enjoyed. After graduation, I found a job that was fun and rewarding, which turned into a more technical computer role. As I began to look at life and evaluate where I was, I saw myself as someone working on a computer in a solitary office cubicle for the rest of my life. I did not see the creative side in me at all, and so I brushed it aside. It was not until events later in my life that I began to embrace the creative side of myself, which had always been there. I just had not been open to seeing this side of myself, because I did not feel it would serve any purpose in accomplishing what society expected of me.

And as I evaluate all of this while reading the book *On Becoming an Artist: Reinventing Yourself Through Mindful Creativity,* maybe - just maybe - I'm more creative than I allow myself to be. In fact, I know I am more creative than I ever let on. I'm just beginning to embrace that creativity and allowing it to be more of who I am, rather than something I pull down off the shelf when I feel like I have the time.

In the book, I am seeing that to be mindful is to be creative, and to be creative is being mindful. Being creative gives us the essence and enjoyment of life that we so deserve. Yet, if we only attempt to use it on occasion, we are missing so much for our lives. Being creative and being mindful is not just for a select few, but it is present in each one of us, if we allow it to be. *(Written on 9/19/09)*

Chapter Eight

Connections

----

*Words, thoughts, actions and feelings
are the many beautiful ways we connect
with those around us. May we always
connect with a smile in our heart.*

Selected Writings

For Those Difficult Moments

Say Something Nice

Connected To My Heart

For Those Difficult Moments

If we watch the news or we live in areas where destruction has occurred, many of us feel moved by the suffering of others. We are compassionate beyond our responsibility, as our hearts connect with those who have been affected. While we work hard to help those in need, we often feel like we just cannot do enough.

I remember when my mom was killed in a car accident, I had people telling me they just didn't know what to say or how to help. When in fact, the greatest gift they had given me was just letting me know they were there and that I had support. I wasn't alone! That very thought meant the world to me.

When we face those difficult times in our life, sometimes just the simple fact of knowing we're not walking this journey alone can make all the difference. It can give a boost to our hope, an injection of energy to our step, and a tear to wash away the pain in our eyes.

So when you know people are facing difficult times around you, realize that there is only so much you can do. However, help in any way you can, keeping in mind that you also need to take care of yourself in the process. But know as well, that just by you being there for someone, even if it is to sit there in quiet stillness, you are giving so much more to them than you may know at that moment.

And if it feels like that still isn't enough, you can always send love and blessings from your heart to theirs. Their heart will receive it and it will be one of the purest forms of service, love, and energy you could ever give to another traveler on this earth. *(Written on 8/30/08)*

Say Something Nice

Do you ever stop and think that we very seldom hear nice things or compliments from those around us? Often in our day, we are slammed with criticisms, critiques, and negative gossip that do nothing to raise our vibrations, our spirit, or our outlook on life. And yet, one of the simplest things we could do for one another on a daily basis is just saying something nice.

I'm not talking about empty meaningless words, for that is no better than the alternative. This has such a big impact on each one of us. The words we use to others and the words we receive from others have so much power.

So why not remember what it felt like when someone said something nice, supportive, caring, or in a manner of thanks, and do a similar thing to someone you meet. You might just completely change their day and their life. It could mean more than the world to them. *(Written on 6/19/09)*

Connected To My Heart

What if I take a moment this morning and just connect - connect with my heart?

What if I feel the love it has to share, the warmth deep inside and the joy it gives in this moment?

What if I just feel that, sense that, and allow it to be one with all of my body, all of my mind, and all of my day?

What if I just hold that throughout the day, breathing in all that is good and exhaling all that I do not need?

What a joy it is that I feel through the lightness of my heart beating, beating, beating as it gives so much to myself and those around me. And just notice in my body, every little thing I can as a result.

Oh Happy Day of Possibilities!

(Written on 5/20/09)

Chapter Nine

Music Connects Us

----

*The sounds of notes drift together to
form music which touches our souls,
enlightens our minds, and carries us
forward with each step as a dance.*

Selected Writings

Music Connects Us
Piano Meditation Music
Multidimensional Music
Relaxation To Yanni

Music Connects Us

Music can lift us from our current plane into a world where nothing matters, where no stress can be found, and where true peace abounds. The individual notes combined together can transcend our hearts and minds.

We all have a favorite song, CD, or band that picks us up when we are down, and energizes us. Have you ever stopped to consider this, and consider just what the music does for you? How does it take you from your current state and leave you feeling fulfilled, ready to fight whatever it is you need to, or just feeling empowered?

I firmly believe that music is the way that the innermost parts of our lives and the universe communicate with us. Music speaks where no words are found. Music creates a language where there is a void. Music knows no boundaries put in place by cultures, governments, or laws.

For a long time in my life, I have played the piano and created music of all kinds. In recent years, I have focused on letting my innermost soul release the sounds that it holds. Just a few years ago, I would find a piano and sit down and play for hours at a time. I never used sheet music as I did not need it. I would just play whatever came out of my fingers. This music was a combination of notes that had never been heard before. And yet I found that I did not really hear the music that I was playing, until one day I recorded a session. When I listened to what I recorded, I could not believe what I heard. I did not realize just what I was creating.

Up to this point, I had not been able to replay anything that I have created. It is as if the music I create is a conversation, and we all know that you can never repeat a conversation once it has been spoken. You can paraphrase it, but there is no way to repeat it. This is why I believe that music which comes from deep within our souls is such a pure form of communication, and it goes where words cannot form.

I began to share my music with a few trusted friends, and saw their reactions. It was at that point that I decided it was time to share my music with the world. The more I have shared the music, the more I have seen the effects of it upon the lives of others. I can see when someone hears it, and it affects them in such a deep way. When someone's ear tunes into the songs I create, I know that they have connected with the deeper language found deep within the music, and they have connected with a much broader source, the Universe.

My music, and the music of many others that I know, comes from a greater source than we find in ourselves. It is the universe that provides this music, and it has the ability to do whatever we need at that moment in our lives. For the universe provides peace, healing, and power to everyone, and one of the ways it does this is through the music that it provides. I've seen how my music reflects the times I am in, and how it has changed as I changed. Each song I create gets a title, so as to keep it separate from the next song, and to reference it to what actually was taking place in my thoughts while it was created.

So as you go about your day, stop for a minute and think about the music you enjoy. What is it trying to tell you? To what is it connecting you? What are your mind and body needing at this very minute? Remember we are all connected to something greater than ourselves, and that connection is kept together by a force called music.

If you have not had an opportunity to hear some of my music, I hope you will take a moment and go to the following link:

http://www.donshetterly.com

(Written on 11/09/05)

Piano Meditation Music

Meditation: the moments you spend in solitude and silence, with reflection and a listening ear. Yet, these moments sometimes seem to me to be some of the hardest things to embrace in any given day. Between everything that is going on and all that I need to get done, the minutes fly by.

Today as I was sitting there playing my piano, I thought back to all the days that this has been a constant in my life. No matter how difficult the days or the events got in my life, there was always the piano. In fact, between the piano and my pets, I could always find life's center. When nothing else in life gives me a moment of peace or stillness, I always have my piano.

When I was a child, my house was never dull and quiet. There were constant times of screaming, yelling, and criticizing. In addition to that, love, touch, and companionship were shown to us in ways that were abusive, harmful, and full of evil. It was in those moments that the only thing I could do was to find a way to escape. I could not deal with what was taking place at that time, and it was not like I could just run away from the situation. There was no place to run to, and no place to hide.

During these times, I would turn to my piano and play the songs that I so loved. Most of these were church hymns and choruses, because that was all I knew and about all I was ever allowed to work with. Their easy melodies and harmonies, along with the gentle and peaceful words found in the verses of the songs, made for some beautiful moments of connectedness for my life.

Today as I was playing some of these songs, I noticed the pain and turmoil of the past being brought up within the notes. The pain and turmoil were as much a connection to these songs for me as the peaceful moments. And while the pain and turmoil are sometimes still overwhelming to me, there is a side of these songs that takes me into a space unlike any other. It is a place of deepness, far removed from this world.

One could say it is a place of meditation or spirituality, but to me it goes much deeper than that. It is very hard to describe. I know I have read that Yanni talks about going into a black space when he creates. I'm sure what he is talking about, and what I'm talking about, are our own similar experiences with this. I'm sure each artist knows firsthand what this space is.

It is a beautiful place to be and travel into. It does give me the opportunity to be deep in meditation. To me, meditation is not only about sitting cross-legged in silence. It is much more than that. Meditation is a deep connection to what is not readily seen or heard. I'm always amazed at just how much insight, awareness, and communication I receive when I'm deep in the meditative moments of playing my piano and creating.

May you find those deep moments within yourself that help you reset, give you renewal, and a different outlook. May your own meditation bring you deeper within yourself.

While I don't record most of what I play in these moments, some of the music has made it on to my CD's of relaxing piano music from the heart. This music often comes out of those times, and sound clips can be found on iTunes, Amazon, Rhapsody or Napster.

For More Information on my music, visit my website at http://www.donshetterly.com *(Written on 4/25/10)*

Multidimensional Music

Music is one of those things, where the love of a particular song lies in the eye of the beholder! No two people have the same musical taste, or likes and dislikes. And music that one person may consider relaxing or invigorating may be like fingernails on a chalkboard to someone else.

When it comes to new age bodywork modalities, the common perception is that it must be non-intrusive music and have a certain sound to it. Without some of the normal nuances one would expect to hear in "spa music", many consider it not worthy to be played with body work.

I remember several clients over the years who have asked that I do massage to all kinds of music from jazz, to classical, to rock, or whatever was playing at the time. At first, I began to wonder how I could do it. Then I realized that the music was for the client, and not necessarily for me.

As I did the massage, I began to notice that I picked up on various beats within the beat of the music, and various sounds within the notes. I used whatever rhythm or musical sounds I needed to help achieve what it was that I was doing at the time. I learned that I could do massage to just about anything, and mix in what I was doing and what the body needed, with what that client was hearing on the table and where they were at in that moment. What came through to my hearing was matching the vibration of the body at that moment.

When I hear a song, whether it is fast or slow, I hear many parts of it. To my ears, there are notes and sounds within the notes of the song. It is what lies *between* the notes that are played that I pick up. One could call this the vibration or resonance of the music. In addition, my ears pick up various layers of the beat or the rhythm of a song. There is the main rhythm of the song, but my ears pick out different beats, or sometimes my ears knock out certain beats -- so in effect, I'm slowing the rhythm down. A song that may sound too fast to some sounds much different to me.

For me, I take it one step further when I'm doing bodywork sessions with clients. I begin to match my movements and what I do with the tempo, or the sounds that their body needs in that particular moment. In the next moments, things may have already changed in their body -- and so then I begin matching the things together again. It is like a flowing melody where the tempo and sounds change, but they match together with the movement and transition of the body. All of this happens automatically without even thinking about what I am doing. If I thought about it, most likely it would not happen as easily because it is just part of where I connect with the client and their body.

Music is more than playing a few notes with a rhythm. It is multidimensional, and if we stop and listen, we will hear something within the music that were not necessarily intended -- but they are part of the song. This gives the richness and fullness to the song, and gives it life that connects from one heart to another. I am very moved by music, and when I've used my own music in bodywork sessions, I've had people tell me that they felt as if my hands were playing their body, just as if I was playing my piano. It was as if I was creating music with the body, just as a musician would do with an instrument.

Here's a homework assignment. Take some music that you would normally listen to, and some that you would not. See if you can pick up the other rhythms and beats within the songs, as well as the notes between the notes. See if you can play with what you hear to achieve a different effect in your own body, or that of a client. It is an amazing experience if you allow yourself the opportunity to do this. It adds so much more to the music experience.
(Written on 3/23/10)

Relaxation To Yanni

I am lying here trying to find a sense of relaxation. Listening to the CD by Yanni, "Live At the Acropolis," I felt as if I was miles above the earth.

There were vast mountains below me with a rippling, flowing stream leading down to a quiet, peaceful lake on the left. To my right, was the sunset in a gorgeous horizon, filled with beauty and splendor. In front of me, rising high into the sky, were the blackest, meanest, and most horrifying storm clouds you have ever seen.

As the music started with its fast tempo, I could see myself flying all around over the earth. Not a thing was holding me down and at that moment in time, I had risen above life and the problems it so freely gave me.

As the music slowed to an eerie tempo, I found myself scared and anxious. Waiting and watching; looking out for someone that may bring harm to me. I was cautious and frightened, not sure where to hide, but knowing I was not ready to go back down to the earth and face the pain.

As the music became a slow, peaceful pace, I could see two large hands coming down from the heavens. These two hands scooped me up with a warm gentle touch that made me feel so safe and secure.

As the music carried on, I rested in the warm safety of these hands. *(Written on 6/02/98)*

Chapter Ten

Listening

If we listen with our hearts, our minds and our bodies, then we will truly hear that which is meant for us.

Selected Writings

Answers Within Us

Listening To The Universe

Ask Your Angels

Hands Of Angels

Angel Of Comfort

Answers Within Us

I keep reading things online that just make me wonder, because I see so many searching for the answers - for the true path - for the way out of whatever circumstance it is that they are facing.

God knows I've been in each of those places and in some ways I continue to struggle with them at varying degrees, throughout different times in my life. And yet, I come back to one truth that has helped me move from where I was, to where I currently am. It is one truth - it is one fact - it is one thing.

That thing for me is that the answers lie within myself. I can go out all day and hunt, search, quest, look for or whatever else one could think of here, but at the end of the day, the answers that I need for my life are within me. I will not find them anywhere beyond me or outside of me or in another person, place, thing, or even through increased money in my pocket.

Don't get me wrong here either - I know that there are people, places and events that have helped draw me closer to the truths that I sought during the times I needed them. They were the angels - the godsends - the wise ones that showed me a nugget of discovery that led me closer to finding the answers that I sought within myself. It might have been a book - it might have been a healer or a song or whatever --- the list of all those that helped me find those nuggets in life could go on and on. At the end of the day, though, the answers that I am seeking are located within me.

We have so much truth within ourselves, and we have too much strength that we know not of. Yet we as humans look outward for these things, when they are not outside of us but inside of us. I know it isn't easy to search within ourselves to find the answers we need, but they are there, if we only look deep enough.

Life should be experienced as a bunch of parts made into a whole. We are the sum total of all those parts, which include our journey, our quest, and our struggle, as well as our happiness, joy, love, inspiration, and so forth. These things are all one and the same. They are not separate. Let us embrace them as all part of the continuum of our life and let us not separate them out into good or bad parts, but parts that help us truly become who we are.

For in each one of us is life, and in life is each one of us. We celebrate our life for who we are, who we are becoming, and how our lives will touch and impact those of our fellow travelers. Let us embrace all that is life and all that we do not currently understand. Let us not stop on the road at what currently confronts us, but let us continue on, taking one step at a time and feeling every part of that which is yearning for our attention.

Sometimes that which takes years to get our attention may appear in ways we do not understand. If we stop and allow ourselves to become one with it, we find the common ground and treat it as our teacher. As we learn together with our teacher, we then discover more of that which we may not currently understand about ourselves.

Let all of this guide us as we go further into our lives, embracing the feelings of pain, loneliness, poverty, sadness, tears and all other things, until we have fully learned from and understood that which they are trying to teach us - that they are trying to help us become more fully aware of ourselves. Let us not stop but let us continue getting to know the innermost details of our beings, our existence, and our lives.

And may we celebrate on the journey, and dance as we've never danced before, through the rough times and the good times, for they are all one and the same - they are us - they are life!

And now let me remind myself of all these things and bow in respect of all who are there helping me learn these intimate details of my own life. *(Written on 8/04/05)*

Listening To The Universe

How much do we miss in our day? It is most likely much more than any one of us wants to admit. The messages are there, but in our culture and society, we've been well trained to just go on in our daily life and sort of ignore them. It is like getting a cell phone call, and then dropping the call. The universe is then saying to us, "can you hear me now?"

While there may be some very gifted people that are meant to connect with the universe in a special way, I believe that anyone can do this. I believe we all can get messages if we are open to them, and allow them to come in. All too often, we close our lives off through fear and shutting down that stream of information we so want.

Isn't it amazing that there is no shortage of people in this world asking questions of what they should do in life? The questions include finances, abundance, relationships, jobs, careers, and purpose in their lives. They often seek out others to tell them what they should be doing in life. While others may help them discover some of their truths, they often give their power up to those people. At the same time, they fail to connect with their own internal message stream.

Things like not trusting one's self, fear, and past experience can muffle the message, or block it out altogether. Staying so busy in our lives, or chasing the wrong rainbow gives us little opportunity to connect. Having low self confidence leaves us doubting all that we experience, wondering if we are trusting a thief in the night or a Good Samaritan. Past trauma and even current-day stress can distort all that we view, and pick up in our days even with the best of intentions.

This information is so valuable to us. It shows up through heart tugs, feelings of ease or difficulty, abundance or lack, body pain and illness, and many other ways. How we feel in our lives is the prompt to evaluate our direction.

If we attempt to hide from the things we need to face, can we expect a good outcome for our daily lives?

Yes, often we are not sure what the next step is. I have been at the point of being physically paralyzed from a conversion disorder (also known as a somatoform disorder), and quite literally did not know how to take the next step. I had to trust that the physical therapist and doctors knew how to help me. I had to have the courage and determination to keep trying, no matter how tough it got, to function once again. I had to allow myself to focus in the moment, and on my body, so that I could recover. Sometimes we do not know what to do, but inaction or doing nothing will get us no further than we are in the moment.

It all starts with quieting our minds, connecting to our bodies, and allowing ourselves to open up and listen. Acknowledge the fears so that you are able to let them go. Let the energy of the fears and pain help motivate the change, instead of allowing it to pull you under. Spend time regularly allowing yourself to stop, rest, and be open. Allow yourself the opportunity to listen. Give yourself the permission.

Then, just observe what thoughts, patterns, or yearnings you notice. See what thoughts pop into your mind and prompt you to take action. See how different events make you feel, and move toward the ones you are passionate about. Let yourself be in the moment, giving yourself the permission to just open up and listen and connect with all that you are. *(Written on 7/13/10)*

Ask Your Angels

While I know there are people who feel angels do exist, I know that there are many who just feel they don't. Frankly, it does not matter to me any longer if people believe what I do on this, because I have been shown countless times in countless ways that they do exist in my life. I know deep down what I sense, and I know there are times that I can claim, without a doubt, to know they were there for me.

Of course, we all see and feel and believe things through our own filters in life. It is up to each of us to search ourselves out and understand what it is that we connect with, and where we may be blocked in connecting with the unseen in life.

One such example happened for me the other day. I've had a situation that has gone on for a long time in my life, and because of some recent situations, it had really kicked up a lot of turmoil for me. Events had progressed to the point where it was consuming way too much of my time and thoughts, and creating a very difficult state within my body.

So finally, during some meditation time that I was having that day, I finally just said, "ok, enough! Angels, I really need your help on this because I really need to let go of this situation and be able to move on in my life. No longer can I continue to think about this situation each day, as it is just too much for me. It is consuming me. I need your help to work through this, and somehow move the situation forward. I'm not asking it to be resolved at this moment, but just to be able to have something change, that allows me to let go of it."

It wasn't but 30 minutes or an hour later that I got a call from a certain person. It had been several weeks since I last had contact from them, and they had completely closed off all communication by phone, letter, and email. No matter what I did, they completely ignored me. This had been going on for many weeks. Things, of course, were not 100% resolved but at least initial contact by phone had been made and they explained some of the recent situations that had happened in their life. I could understand all they had been through recently and that they had shut down the communication, not because they wanted to, but because it was just part of their process.

I'm still amazed that this happened so quickly. Time and time again, I've been told to ask my angels for the things I need help with, because they are ready to help us. I keep forgetting to do this, even though this is not the first time I've seen quick results like I did. It is wonderful to know that we are all connected to so much more than we can see.

Unfortunately, so many doubt these things because of the people in the public spotlight that cast doubts upon what is possible. May we all open our eyes a little further in what we see, and may we all question what is real, what it is that we feel and sense, and what we have yet to understand. *(Written on 5/24/10)*

Hands Of Angels

Last night as I went to bed, I was filled with so many ordeals that I had been through in the past week: situations that were very stressful, painful at times, and overall exhausting. I felt as if the universe had given me too much, and comfort was extremely difficult to come by. My mind was racing and I knew that somehow, I needed a rest from this. I needed comfort and safety and just knowing I wasn't alone.

It was at that moment, that I sensed the angels around me. I could feel them, many in numbers. Startled by what felt like hands lying firmly on my back as I lay in bed, I jumped to look around and noticed that no one was touching me. The hands lying on my back were not oppressive but calming, reassuring and gentle. As I tried to just relax and let go, I felt more hands, too numerous to count on my back. Again, I jumped up to see who was touching me, and there was no one.

I knew deep down that there were many angels around me, all with their hands on my back as if to say, "we are all here for you - you are not alone." I noticed the warmth and the heat generated where the hands were touching, and it felt so supportive and so filled with love. It gave me a great sense of relief knowing that there was something watching over me. Their hands of love gave me assurance that I am not alone, and all this that has been given to me will pass.

So in thankful adoration to the angels who were there for me, I lovingly accept your hands of encouragement, support, and a calming reassurance to me. Thank you for being there for me. I will hold this in my thoughts and in my heart for when I feel the burdens are too great. *(Written on 4/25/10)*

Angel Of Comfort

Yesterday I was at a low point in life feeling completely and utterly worthless, and that no one wanted me because how could anyone want me - the way I felt about myself. This had been building, but had gotten to the point where I found the courage to tell Jeff that I didn't think he wanted me anymore, either. Of course I figured he was going to say that I truly was worthless and of course, he didn't want me. (Not that Jeff would do this, but my mind had me believing that this would happen because it was the threat that was always played upon me growing up.) Once I said this to Jeff, he replied that it may have more to do with how I see myself than anything else right now.

I was thinking, "Well, what kind of response is that?" That's not what I expected to hear. "How dare you not play things out like my mind believes things are supposed to go? Just who gives you the right to change the game plan?" That's how my mind was thinking and while I can hear anyone saying, "Well he wouldn't do that," you're most likely correct. But you couldn't convince my mind of that at the time.

And as we talked last night, it became clear that while I so badly wanted to be touched by Jeff, what he felt was a wall that I had put up. I know I do put walls up and at the same time, I want someone to care. Don't ask me to explain - I just know I do it!

So tonight at the session with Dr. Canali, I brought up that Jeff and I had a big talk the night before, and so we spent some time talking. It helped because normally, as I had been taught in some dramatic ways, you were not allowed to talk to anyone about situations such as a relationship. That was a complete no no. So this was a good thing, and it didn't cause anyone to leave, or any bad thing to happen.

Then during the session, I started out like normal, not really sensing much of anything in my body, and Dr. Canali encouraged me to sense and to feel my body. As I did this, I began to notice tightness in my shoulders and upper back. I could begin feeling how the breath would get to this point, and then with the restrictions it didn't want to go very much further. And the more I focused on it, the more I realized just how painful it was. I spent much time moving and feeling the pain and for one of the first times ever, not afraid to go in and do this. I could feel the fear in the back and shoulders, but I felt it was time to go here and I felt safe, supported and loved. Compare that to the previous day!

It wasn't until I turned over on my back that I really began to realize I was in a very deep place. I was aware of some things around me, but not really. And the place I was in, seemed so far away from everyday life. I could feel a strong presence like an angel hovering over me as if there was a nice warm soft blanket resting upon me. It was a very comforting feeling and warming feeling. I'm going to refer to it as an angel because I think that is what it was. Dr Canali didn't come around for awhile, until the angel had stepped away from me. Otherwise they would have been in each other's way.

And with all of this, I felt safe enough to go further into what I needed to do. My focus began to move toward my stomach and I felt some very tender areas. They were areas of turmoil and pain. It didn't take too long before Dr. Canali came and focused on these areas, which were by then extremely painful. I began to breathe into where his touch was going, instead of turning away from the pain. It took a lot of strength because the fear and the pain were so great. Eventually he took an energy ball and placed it under my hands, which allowed me to regulate the pressure and breathe a little more precisely.

As I allowed myself to go further into the pain, I began touching a very deep place within myself. This went back to a very early age of when I was just an infant. There weren't many thoughts going through my mind, but a single one of when I was first born and was left all alone in the hospital, apart from my family and my mother, to be cared for by the nurses. This was done because my dad had hepatitis, I was told, and my mom had to choose between seeing me and seeing him. Because of his manipulation of my mom, she chose him. Right or wrong, she chose him.

With the thought of this racing through my mind, the sadness came up within me of being left alone, away from my mother and having no one except some nurses to care for me. I found myself through the tears that were flowing from my eyes at this time, saying, "Why, why didn't you stay with me. Why did you leave me?" Of course there are no answers, and my adult mind can see this more clearly, but the child mind just never got over this. There was nothing the child could do, and no one to listen to him at the time. The child had no way to say to anyone what he needed either, for this was a pre-talking stage of his life.

Dr. Canali continued to work with me and at one point I felt myself screaming as loud as I could, with a force coming from deep within until I felt my body just sink down into his arms and back on the table. It was like I went up against the fear, realized I had the power to overcome it, and then just let go with the sinking of my body. It was a very powerful moment and I could feel the energy pulsate throughout my body. I wasn't sure at first what was going on and almost grew afraid of it, but soon realized, it was just energy flowing through me.

My tears turned to joy as I found that somehow I've managed to make it to this point. With everything that was done to me, I've still managed to survive and come as far as I have through life. My tears were of myself telling my body that I loved me, and I was glad to get to know me a little more.

During my New Years Eve walk, where I was walking in desperation, I asked that if angels did exist and they truly cared, that I needed to be comforted and shown care, comfort, and compassion. I have been shown that in so many ways and tonight, the angels that visited me while I was in the session were doing just that. And on the way home, my XM satellite radio played a song called "Angel of Comfort". It was such a short song, which surprised me, but it was amazing that it came on during the drive home. *(Written on 1/09/06)*

Chapter Eleven

Abundance

Connected to your source, through the heart, which allows you to enjoy the overflowing, plentiful consciousness that is present around you.

Selected Writings

We've Got So Much

The Gratitude Jar

Picturing Power Of Our Mind

Creating Our Moments

Thankful Abundance In Our Life

It Is Our Moment

Abundant Day Of Blessings

Allowing Good Things In Our Life

We've Got So Much

Sometimes in life, we look around and complain about many things. We wish this was different or that was different. Sometimes we subscribe to different schools of thoughts, and we know that if we just believe, things will somehow change for the better.

The only thing is while doing this, we often fail to see what is so good about our lives in the current moment. We've already got much more than we sometimes see. We've already accomplished so many of our wishes. We have already changed so much of what we wish to change.

Yet, we are too busy looking for the golden rainbow to notice that the rain and thunderstorms in our lives are actually offering to us what we desire. Sure, we may have to dodge the lightning bolts and the hail and find shelter from the drenching downpours of rain, but just as we celebrate a sunny day, so should we celebrate the rainy season.

Spend time today, observing in your life just all that has come into your life. Recognize what is already there, and what has shown up. Know that life is about seeing what is before us instead of squinting into the horizon to guess at what is out there. *(Written on 6/19/10)*

The Gratitude Jar

Lately, there has been a shift in me, and while it still may be a subtle shift that others haven't seen, I feel it within myself. I can't point a finger directly to the moment, or color the picture exactly as it appeared, but I know it happened and I know it is. The shift has been a long time coming to me and is one that I've been fearful of, yet has wanted to embrace me.

Out of this shift, I am beginning to understand just how important our thoughts are to everything that happens in our day. It wasn't that long ago that I would have said, "Right - hogwash - this ain't reality." But I'm beginning to understand and be taught in the gentlest of ways that this is pure truth. It really is that hard or that simple. Of course this is my own growth, and I can't ask anyone else to believe this until you've pondered its truth for your own life. Only then will the truth be shown to you.

One thing I started back up (although in a different form) was my gratitude list. Jeff and I used to do this at night before we went to bed, and while I feel that was correct for that time, I found myself struggling to remember all the grateful moments of the day. So this time I changed how I am doing this.

I have put a large see-through jar (think it was an animal crackers jar before) right next to my desk, where I can see it at every moment when I'm on the computer. I've got a lot of little pieces of paper cut up and in a location within arm's reach of the jar. So as I find the grateful moments during the day, I take a piece of paper, write them down, and then sign it with the date.

There are a few things I want this to give me. When I'm thinking things are going rough, I want to be able to look at my container and see just how many things make me grateful. I want to do this throughout the day so that my thoughts focus more on that which I'm grateful for, and less on that which is nothing more than negative thoughts for me. I'm anxious to see my jar fill up, and then go back and read all the things that maybe will be hard to remember.

So my challenge to you today is if you want to give your life one heck of a boost, make yourself a gratitude jar! Find a clear see through container and keep it somewhere that you will see it most frequently. Keep some spare pieces of paper and a pen close by, so that you can add your little gratitude moments to it without any effort whatsoever. And then watch it grow and become who you are! Try it for a month or two and see just how it affects your life. I'd love to hear from people who do this and I'd love to hear the effects it has had on your life.

And may love and peace come to you at some moment during this day. *(Written on 8/27/07)*

Picturing Power Of Our Mind

My mind has always been creating, and I constantly see images and scenes that sometimes play like a movie that you see at a theater. Often as a child in school, my mind would create a ton of image scenarios as if I was writing a book or directing a movie. Some people would most likely refer to it as daydreaming and some might say it is an overactive mind. It could be both of those, but the important thing is my mind does this about as easily as my lungs take a breath of air.

There were many times before painting our house, I would see the colors we had chosen on the wall. When we were buying home decor, in my mind I would see where each of the decor items would be and how they would fit. I often plan events or projects or even things I write in my mind first, before step one is ever begun. When I drive, I do so more by the images of my route than remembering the roads I turn on, especially if I have already traveled this route before.

I forget, sometimes, that I can consciously use the imaging in my mind to create that which I want to move toward in my life. Picturing images in my mind occurs unconsciously, and yet consciously I can use the same process.

For a moment, think about something you want to achieve. It could be a task, a project, or maybe something you want to be different in your life. It could be a health or financial condition, or something as simple as a repair problem you are facing. While you may not be able to picture all the steps in the process of what you want, that is not important. Instead create the outcome in your mind of what you do want. Pull in images, colors, sights, sounds and smells in your mind that give you that which you desire. Make the image of what you want so vivid that it is almost as if you're living it in that moment.

As you do this, begin to let it absorb into every part of your being, including your mind, soul, body, and senses. Feel every part of it. Sense every part of it. When you do this, things may come up in your life that need to be cleared out of the way to make this happen. These things could be significant or they could be very small and unnoticeable, like fears, thought patterns, lifestyle. Whatever it is, listen to that in your body and in your mind. Take the necessary steps to clear, clean and further embrace the image you are picturing in your mind.

You may notice as you more fully embrace the image that it may need to change, or you may see something you did not see before. Take note of that and add it into your picture. Make it a part of all that you feel, sense, and see.

Don't just stop at the picture part either, but really feel that all of this has happened and that you are grateful for it. Give thanks for what you have imaged as if it has already happened, for you are creating all that you can have and that which is part of your entire self.

We all create our realities in a day, whether they be forward and positive, or draining and caught in events that have already passed us by. Sometimes we are conscious of this and sometimes it goes unseen. So make the most of your day by picturing what you want for your life, and being thankful as if it already happened. *(Written on 6/02/09)*

Creating Our Moments

Some days I wonder about my life and where it is heading. While I can see specific steps in my path, it seems there is just so much that I haven't discovered, as if I'm at the beginning of the journey. In some ways that is most likely true, and in other ways it feels as if I've been walking for many lifetimes, almost as if this isn't the first time through this journey.

But as I know, all things that I encounter and all the experiences I have had up to this point in my life, have made me what I am today. It is the sum of all the parts of myself with the good, the bad, and the pieces I would greatly like to discard. Without any of these parts, I would not be who I am today or where I am. Each part played a role in getting me to this one moment in time that I am at today. And so, while I revel in the great moments of my life and the great experiences I have had, it is those dreaded parts that have been just as momentous for me.

The other day I was thinking that I really had not done enough for others around me. I felt as if I didn't really have anything to offer those around me in my community or the world. I felt inadequate with just not having enough; a mindset of lack, not of abundance, even though I know I've been so blessed in so many ways.

Than it struck a chord with me, just as if I put my fingers on the keyboard. I was not lacking and inadequate and failing others. In fact, this past year, I've helped some people out, selling an estate collection for them. Even though I knew very little about this, my job was to do the physical work to get it sold. Others around me knew the ins and outs of doing this, and so their help and assistance made it all possible.

More importantly though is that the people I was selling this for, like myself, were in dire straits and needed the extra income. The extra income helped each party make it through a year that would have been even harder to get through. The timing of how these things came together was not of this world, because it all happened at the right moment and with the right set of circumstances.

So as I thought about all of this, I realized that I was not giving myself credit for all I had done. That's not unusual for me, and it is one of those things in my life, I'd love to give up. It is my beloved and hated twin – that of not giving myself credit. If I would have not done my part in this scenario, then not only would I have suffered but so would others involved with it. They would have been deprived of something that greatly helped them through a very difficult year.

Maybe sometimes we don't need to put helping others, and being there for others, in a nonprofit organization sort of way. Maybe these things come in all shapes and sizes, and allow us to be enhanced in life while we help others. After all, it doesn't have to be one or the other. It could be both!

Putting this in perspective, I can now look back at the previous year and see things that weren't obvious to me each day. I can now look back and know that I did add to the overall good of others, the community, and our world, while I also helped myself along. I can now look back and realize that my skills and time used to do this were exactly what was needed. Nothing more! Nothing less! Those skills don't say lack either. They are abundance, because they gave so much to so many.

Sometimes we want to fit life into our own little molds, and through our filtered eyes, view it as a picture film already created. We fail to see that our life has not been designed, but is created with each passing moment. It is in the individual moments that life is lived to the fullest, not in the unrealistic expectations that we may place upon ourselves.

And we can always know that if what we created today is not what we wanted it to be, that we can always create something different tomorrow. Tomorrow will always be a clean slate for us. The important part is to create and live in the moment we have right now. *(Written on 1/25/09)*

Thankful Abundance In Life

I'm thankful today, for all I've been given.

I'm thankful for all I've been given in life. This includes the pain, the bad stuff, and the difficult lessons of life.

I'm thankful for the supportive and caring people around me. I feel the love so strong in this moment.

I'm thankful for those who showed me harm in my life, for they have helped me grow in ways I most likely would not have.

I'm thankful for the beauty that is all around me. This includes those parts of our world that cast shadows in the night and darkness during the day, for it shows that light is all around me.

I'm thankful for the sounds and music around me. I hear the screams and the silence but together they show me the full width of the sound spectrum.

I'm thankful for restful moments in my life. They bring moments of reflection through the confusion of stress.

I'm thankful for my fears in life. For my fears and discomfort give way to showing me areas of growth in my life and helping to keep my feet on the path.

I'm thankful for everything in my life. I realize all the events that swirl around me like a tornado, will lead to days of sunshine and calm.

I'm thankful today, for all I've been given. I'm truly blessed.
(Written on 7/05/10)

It Is Our Moment

Every day we wake up into a world that has not been created at that moment. It is each waking moment, each step we take, and each thought we derive, that creates our day. What we choose to do with it and how we choose to live it, is our choice and our choice alone. In this moment, no one in our past, present, or future, can create the day for us. While others may influence and impact it, the choices we make are still up to us.

Yet for so many of us, we go through life feeling as if events and circumstances are in control of who we are. We are blown by various winds in our day, drenched by the storms, and drawn to pretty colored fake neon signs. These things take our eyes off our path and draw us away from why we are here.

May we be like a ship coming into the harbor, watching the beacon from the lighthouse that illuminates the path ahead. May we not lose sight, watching the lightning from the storm, and run aground into the rocks.

(Written on 6/27/09)

Abundant Day Of Blessings

It was truly one of those days. Just hours earlier, I was really feeling pretty roughed up in life, struggling to make sense of some things. They tend to be normal things, but nevertheless they are my beloved and hated twins. Most of the time, I can tough it out, act strong and act as a man while muddying through it. This day, though, things were just building a little too much for me.

So I had some alone time and I sat and talked to the angels, as I call it. Most people may think I am a little strange here, or if they saw me they might think I was really losing my marbles, because it would appear I was talking with no one. Call it what you may or what you must, but to me it is talking to my angels.

Anyway, I expressed my concerns, frustrations and anger. Normally, I don't hold back and I just say it as I see fit. It is what seems natural and normal to me. I do remember when people used to tell me in church, you shouldn't get mad and scream at God. Oh really. Well, if God or the angels or the universe (however you look at it) aren't big enough to handle all of this, than they really aren't that powerful and wonderful in my eyes. I digress though.

So yesterday we went to check out a massage school. I wanted to make another contact in the area, get a small bottle of massage oil, and check on CEU classes. While we were getting ready, a thought popped in to my mind to go to the store, Guitar Center, and see about an audio interface for recording music. You see, since I got my new laptop, I have been struggling to record music from my keyboard onto it with a good quality sound. When I bought the laptop, little did I know that together, Dell and Microsoft and the Recording Industry, would try to prevent something as simple as this. I've spent more hours than I want to think of trying to resolve this.

Anyway, back to the journey. The massage school was different than what I was used to, and no classes were in session, but I found the massage oil I wanted and got some information. It was a nice connection but I really do miss Educating Hands, the school in Miami that I attended.

We then headed to Guitar Center, and when I showed the sales person what I was after, he said, "that is not going to do well for what you are doing." I'm like, okay... so what will, that isn't real expensive, because some of these items get pretty expensive. He pulled out a cheaper one, but it would only allow me to record one channel in stereo, which wasn't ideal. Then I asked him what the best solution is, and he pulled out another which was about $50 more. I'm thinking okay... I record music. I want to do this and I want it to be right. Of course, the business account didn't have enough to cover it, but there's always plastic, right? So I then noticed there was a discount from a couple of places connected to my music distribution. At first, he didn't think either of them qualified for a discount but went to the computer, punched in a few keys and said, I can give you a discount of $25. I'm like...cool. I'll buy it! Later when I checked online, neither of these music services I mentioned had any discount with this place. He didn't have to give me the discount but he did. I'll finish the rest of that story in a moment.

So on the way home, I got a call from a good friend of mine who works with Dr. Canali. I've been struggling lately to find others who are consciously aware of life in the way that I am, and Dr. Canali is. I've missed him and my friend a lot, and I just needed that connection. Right now, to make a trip to Miami, hotels are at the peak of the season and are extremely expensive. So it really isn't an option at the moment. Anyway I found out they were coming to a place about 90 miles from us this weekend to do a seminar/workshop for another therapist I know. I'm like...smiles, hi 5's and the whole works! Just to reconnect with them and be around this will be worth more than a government bailout package! I had tears in my eyes just knowing that I would get to see them again. These are two people who have been with me through so much and along to Jeff, they hold a very special place in my heart.

Anyway, I got home and told Jeff I needed to try out the massage oil. Of course he happily agreed to let me try it out on him. I gave him a 45 minute back massage, which I haven't done on anyone in some time. I was kind of amazed that I still remembered what to do, but when I finished, you could see it in his face that not only did he enjoy it but he was relaxed. A big confidence booster it was, just knowing that I still had the touch.

So on through the rest of the story. I got home and started to hook up the new audio interface to my computer, not really sure what I was doing. Jeff helped me with moral support. And then it happened! I recorded the first sounds through the new device and when I listened to the recorded sound, I was blown away. The sound was so crisp, clear, and of a quality that I had never heard come out of a recording before. It was beautiful and I have a feeling this will give me the added edge my music has been lacking. I knew it was missing something, but I didn't realize what I had been missing all this time. I'm glad I struggled through this issue and ended up buying the device that I bought. It was like it was meant to be and I was just a little slow to figure it out!

As I was thinking, though, when I went to bed last night, so many things happen in our days and if we're not careful, they will pass us by without even noticing them. The joys from yesterday were great and were the pick-me-up I needed. They were the confidence booster, the new insight, the revolutionized way of creating future music! They were examples of knowing that I'm not alone and that I have so much support out there. It was a day of letting me know, that they, the angels, are listening. Indeed it was an abundant day of blessings. *(Written on 3/04/09)*

Allowing Good Things In Our Life

Allowing things to happen in the way they need to is often easier to say than it is to do. It is easy to think that we do allow things in our lives, but if we are truly honest with ourselves, we do often hold back. It is part of our human nature.

Many times, we ask for things in our life, whether it is money to pay the bills, abundance in our life, a new job, or other changes we desire and need. We visualize and we pray and we talk about all of these things but yet, they never seem to show up. We then become discouraged thinking that we are not good enough to deserve these things, and that is why they are not showing up.

When they do try to show up in our consciousness, we are often so busy self-sabotaging our lives that we don't see these things. It has been said that what we need for our lives is around us and within us. All we have to do is tap into it, turn it on, and allow it to come into full view.

One recent example within myself is that I was desiring the opportunity to do something I loved to do. Over and over I hoped for it, wished for it, and tried hard to visualize it. I felt as if I was not getting anywhere. All of the sudden, my mind had one of those light bulb moments, where I realized that I already had what I needed for the opportunity I was seeking. All I had to do was to put it together. It was there all the time, but since I was spending my energy hoping for it, I was missing what was there. I was not allowing it to unfold and happen.

Allowing is not always an easy thing for humans to do. We want to give ourselves the fake illusion that we are in control. We need nothing else because we are all powerful. It is true that we are powerful beyond comprehension, but when that power turns into a road block for our lives, it holds us back from allowing things to happen. There is a difference between the power that helps move us forward and the power that is from the ego.

To allow good things and the things we desire to come into our stream of consciousness, we need only to stop and search deep within. We are already engulfed in so many wonderful things. We just need to stop, seek, and find. Yes, it most likely will entail great personal growth, but without that, we do not evolve as humans.

Take a moment throughout today and your days ahead to notice where you focus your energy. We all have things we must do in a day, and sometimes what we feel we must do is not as it appears. Look at where your focus goes. Is this feeding the route to which you desire to go? Is it bringing you closer to what you seek in life? Is your life filled with ease and is it flowing?

Then, consider how you might change the slightest thing in your life that will bring your energy and focus in line with your desires. It could be a shift of thought and outlook. It could be a change in something you do in your day. It could be asking a simple question such as "how do I allow this into my life?" There are many things you could do, and the possibilities are endless.

There is that part of us located deep within our body that is our compass and barometer. It prompts us to go forward, to listen to connections in life, and help us find lighting for our path. If we tap into this powerful force within us, it will not only help us to become more consciously aware, but will help us tap into that place of allowing things to happen in our life. It is our connection to the stream of consciousness we have for our lives. May we allow it. *(Written on 7/19/10)*

Chapter Twelve

Special Moments

Sharing one's life with the world allows the writer to experience their moments, in a much deeper and connected way than just allowing them to drift by.

Selected Writings

The Easter Lily

Behind The Christmas Glitter

From Paralysis and Fear Through Touch

A Little Boy, A Big Piano

A Tribute To My Mom

Breathe

The Easter Lily

As a kid I was always doing things for my mom, because she was the only older person in my life that wasn't abusing me every day. She seemed to understand me and she accepted me. If I was able to experience anything close to love while growing up, it would have been the love she had for me. We were so much alike in so many ways. We were both extremely sensitive and very intuitive when it came to life. We could both sense things and just see through the small little trials of the day, into a bigger picture. And we were both tormented by the monster each day, who treated us as if we were less than.

I remember one time when I was very young, and on my way home. I went by a tree and broke off a branch full of what I thought were flowers. They were so pretty and smelled so good. I rushed home because I wanted to give them to my mom. Of course when I got home and my mom saw them, I remember her eyes lighting up and a smile coming to her face. She was thrilled to get them, and found a gentle way to let me know that they were from an apple tree. They weren't necessarily the flowers I thought they were, as they were just blossoms from a flower tree. Anyway, my mom put them in a vase and let the fragrance fill the air.

Holidays were always a special time with us. At Easter, my mom would always fix a nice big basket of Easter candy and set it out for us in the morning. There was never a year that was forgotten or missed, and age didn't matter. One of the things that I started doing for my mom as a kid was to take some of the money I earned from my paper route, and go buy her the most beautiful Easter Lily I could find on Easter Sunday. She was always so happy to get this, and I think it really brought a smile to her, even in future years when she knew she would probably be getting one. Few words were ever spoken on this, but I knew deep down what it meant to her. It seemed my dad never got her flowers (that I can remember), but it was my way of saying to her that she was a special part of my life.

Years have gone by, and this practice stopped once I left home. The last flowers I bought for my mom were for the last day I would ever see her again. They were beautiful flowers, full of energy and full of love, just for her. I wish she was still around right now, so that I could go out and buy another Easter Lily for her. I may just go to the store and buy one to celebrate what she did give to me in life. Oh how I miss her so much, but today at least I know through the tears, I can celebrate an Easter lily together.

Mom, I'm going to get you an Easter lily.

(Written on 4/22/03)

Behind The Christmas Glitter

This is actually the first year in many that I've not dreaded Christmas. Normally at this time of the year, my body is aching, stiff, and sore, and I want to hide or lash out at anyone I see, especially in the stores. But this year, it's been different for some reason. Not that I'm doing anything different in my activities, but maybe that part of me is beginning to heal.

Normally depression hits me so hard that I struggle to keep my head above water. I remember a few very recent Christmas times that just about pulled me under. A couple of years ago, I almost lost it in a Kmart shopping lot, on an unsuspecting shopper. That really woke me up a bit. Then I went into hiding, wanting to just end things. It was a tough year. So like I was saying, something has changed.

Granted, it's not all fun and giggles. I get irritated when I see people spending countless hundreds (thousands) of dollars on gifts that are going to end up in yard sales, or the garbage, a few months later -- just to prove to someone they love them. I get irritated when I try to go to the store for something we need, and everyone acts as if the world was ending tomorrow and you'd never be able to buy another thing.

I remember those times when people invited me over for Christmas, and I felt so awkward. While I know they cared, and they were offering their home and goodwill, it was some rough moments. Again, though, I remember when no one invited me over and I sat at home, missing everything in life and hating everything there was to hate. Those times were difficult and if you turned on a TV or a radio, all you heard or saw was about Christmas. If you just happened to catch your neighbors through the window, you could see they were off celebrating with family, or someone was coming to their home bringing presents in the door. There was no escaping it.

From the time I was a little kid, there was one time of year that was special in our house. My mom made sure of it. It was Christmas. We never had much, and we barely got any gifts. I could never understand for the longest time how Santa would bring many gifts to my friends, but not to us. Then when I learned who Santa really was, I found out how my mom saved her pennies up all year long to buy a few gifts for each of us.

She made it special with her baking of holiday treats, with helping put together a Christmas program at church, and by decorating the house. I'll never forget that about her. There were, of course, the rough moments mixed in, when we would exchange gifts as I got older. Sometimes the gift wasn't perfect enough for the person, and you would see and hear the disappointment in them. That grew difficult to accept, and to this day I still struggle when receiving gifts and giving them. I worry so much if the person will like them, or if I will disappoint them.

There is no easy way to deal with this time of year. Each person has their own perceptions of what Christmas should be, and it is rooted in what it was when they were a kid. While it is supposed to be one of the happiest times of the year, I know personally just how tormenting it can be. I've learned over the years to do what I need to do for myself, and push aside all the things that others feel I must do.

As time has passed, I have begun to create a Christmas time that works for me, as I borrow from all my experiences, and as I lean onto that which I truly feel like doing in a year. And yet I know, whatever I do will be enough for me to enjoy or tolerate Christmas in whatever way I so desire. I am not obligated to do Christmas, just because it is that time of year. The only thing that matters is that I take care of myself and nurture the little boy inside of me. *(Written on 12/25/08)*

From Paralysis And Fear Through Touch

Imagine a 25 year old guy lying in a hospital bed and struggling to talk, move all parts of his body, and remember basic things like his name. There was no car accident and no disease. The muscles had the same tone in them as they had before this time.

Just days before, this same guy had been an average hard working person just trying to make it in life. Of course he had the usual aches and pains that everyone has, and he had been getting medical attention to deal with all of this. Of course most of the doctors didn't have the slightest clue what to do in this situation. After a severe episode of seizures, he was taken by ambulance to the hospital, only to be sent home because they found nothing wrong with him.

As the situation worsened, family and friends once again took him to seek additional medical help. Fortunately this time a neurologist knew to ask the right questions, which began the road of healing for this young man. He had been diagnosed with a condition known as a conversion disorder.

Conversion disorders are technically known as somatoform disorders, which involve physical bodily symptoms that suggest there is a medical problem, when in fact no medical condition can be found. Symptoms may include anything from chronic pain, blindness, and deafness, to paralysis of the arms and legs, and seizures. Conversion disorders are estimated to occur in about 15 out of 100,000 people. It is a very rare condition.

If you have not figured out by now who this person is, it was me. I suffered through this condition in 1991 and have fought hard to overcome the effects of it. Although some sources indicate there is no treatment for the disorder, most people would not be able to tell I suffered through paralysis to the point that my brain was shutting down on me.

As part of my continued healing, I spent many years undergoing counseling and therapy to overcome the effects of this condition. With conversion disorders, there is usually an underlying emotional situation, such as child abuse, that goes to the root cause. I did suffer through intense child abuse as a kid, and I have had to deal with the effects that this brought into my life.

For a long time in my life, I struggled with touch. Since my body was beaten and sexually abused as a kid, touch and closeness to other humans were not comforting to me. Yet at the same time, I longed for touch, and I longed to be close to people because it was a very lonely life.

Several years ago, I started trying to receive massage from a very good licensed massage therapist in NC. This lady was very professional, and tried to make sure she could do whatever it took to help me begin accepting touch as something good, healthy, and beneficial. I think I made it through about three sessions, before what she was doing just triggered me to past events. I still remember leaving her office that day, so silent and withdrawn, not able to say what was going on, and afraid of her even though she was doing a fantastic job. Of course it was not her that I was afraid of, it was the touch.

More healing took place in my life, which allowed me for the first time to accept touch in a healthy and wholesome way. As time passed, I began to trust a very special person in my life and touch became so much easier than it had ever been before. However, I went through some very intense periods where a hug would leave me feeling nauseated, and I would feel at times like my skin was crawling with bugs. Even with all of the struggles I faced, my body longed to be touched, and to actually feel the touch and feel the goodness that it held.

After a life-changing event, where I lost my mom to a car accident, I began to contemplate the future direction of my life and the role the universe was asking me to play in it. Amazingly, with all of the touch issues I struggled with, I was drawn to massage school. Just before massage school, I once again had a massage, and it was actually something that was a much more enjoyable experience for me. I knew that

I was drawn to massage school for some reason, but was not totally sure why at that point -- nor was I sure if I could handle learning how to touch others. Fortunately, I trusted my intuition enough and took a giant leap of faith into massage school.

I felt so at home at Educating Hands School of Massage, and I felt as if I would be able to learn how to trust others. So as time passed and we began doing touch on each other, I was so frightened. My body didn't know how to take all of this and so most of the time, it just shut down to what I was feeling. I know several of my classmates were frustrated when we tried to give feedback about the massage, and I had no words to describe it because I could not feel it. I knew that the massage was not bad, but I absolutely could not feel it.

With time and continued massage, day after day, my body began to wake up. It started to see for the first time in my entire life just what touch was. It was like a miracle to me, and as I began to feel the touch of my classmates in my body, I began to feel and sense through my fingers wonderful things that were going on inside of those people I got to work on. As school progressed and the experiences continued to come my way, my body became more awake and alive. Life started to change in dramatic ways for me.

Last July, I again followed intuition and attended a workshop by Dr. Paul Canali on the Enteric Brain. It was at this workshop that I heard someone speak a language about the body which my body fully understood, and realized that no one else had ever spoken in this way. Through my continued work with Dr. Canali's "Unified Healing Therapy", I am for the first time in my life becoming totally aware of what it means to live in my body. I'm actually experiencing what it means to reach a relaxed state, far from the anxiety, depression, and abuse that I suffered from all of my life. Touch is becoming so much more alive in me, and life is becoming more beautiful with each new day of awareness.

Working with people who struggle with touch takes a great deal of patience, understanding, compassion, sensitivity, and non judgment. There are others out there like myself who are afraid of massage and touch. I hope that you realize from my story that while touch is sometimes a very scary thing, you may just be one of the healing stones for that person on their journey. From firsthand experience, I know there is hope for each and every one of these people, and while the journey may get rough, it is well worth it in the end. *(Written on 3/01/05)*

A Little Boy, A Big Piano

I would like to tell you about myself when I was eight years old. I knew that my little fingers were made for something far beyond this everyday existence. Our family had just moved to a small town called Hampton, Iowa. While in the second grade, I knew that I wanted to play the piano. I had never taken a lesson in my short life and I did not know anyone who was an accomplished pianist. Somehow, I just knew that music was a part of me and that I was a part of music. Although I was still discovering this side of myself, the only thing that I did know for certain was that I had a strong desire to play the piano.

Our family had very little money, and the money we had went to buy food, clothes, and to provide a warm place to live. It was not an easy life for me or my family but it was the only one I knew. I knew that even used pianos cost so much and that the likelihood of getting one was very remote. The chances were not good, and so I hoped and prayed every day that I would get a piano. My mom knew how much I wanted a piano, and little did I know at the time, how important it was to her as well.

My mom always wanted to play the piano as a little girl, but her father was against it and would not have anything to do with it. She begged her father to buy her a piano and let her learn how to play the piano. At every turn, she was told "no" because her father needed his money for his alcohol and would not spare any for her to follow the desires of her heart.

So when I expressed to my mom the desire I had to play the piano, she knew that she would not allow the same mistake that her father had made. She knew that if her son truly wanted to play the piano that she was going to help him fulfill this dream, no matter what it took. One day after I came home from school, she gave me the surprise announcement that a neighbor across the street had an old piano for sale. The neighbors only wanted $35 for it.

The piano was a very tall, heavy, and big piano. It had ivory keys and a sound that carried all the way to the distant stars. Sure, it needed to be tuned, but the quality of the sound that came from its keys was more beautiful than any orchestra one could ever hear. It was a sound all to itself, and one that had not been fully utilized. My family loaded the piano up and brought it to its new home, where it would live and sing for many years to come as the little boy brought it to life.

It didn't take long for them to get the piano inside, and my ears heard something coming from the keys as if someone already knew how to play the piano. I found out that even though my mom had never taken a lesson in her life, her hands understood the language of the keys on the piano. She could sit down and hear songs, then play them on the piano. Usually it was only with one hand and she so badly desired to learn how to play, but the responsibilities of her life prevented her from doing this.

Shortly after they got the piano home, I found an elderly lady (Mrs. Ann Tucker) to begin teaching me how to play this magnificent instrument. She taught me how to do everything that I would need to know. All of the basics were there, along with all the disciplines as well. I practiced hard and long, for I wanted to learn everything that I could about the piano. I wanted to make beautiful music with it, and knew that it would take time to learn all the things I needed to learn.

As time passed, I continued to practice the piano every day. I would watch others play the piano and learn as much as I could from what they did. I was always in tune to the sounds they were making, and tried to recreate those sounds. It didn't take long before I started to perform for school choirs, and play in churches.

I continued playing through many years of my life where there was great turmoil. My father was not always appreciative of what I could do, or accepting. Usually my father was very critical of all that I played. One instance I remembered was when my father said, "that song was full of mistakes." To which I replied, "But how can it be full of mistakes? I just created it." And that was the beginning of learning how to make music, and to play the music that was inside of me. It was not music that I could write down, but music that kept coming from deep within.

For many years, this music seemed to have no place, and I did not trust that which was within me. I felt much safer if I could practice a song and memorize it, and then perform it. But for me to allow myself to be the instrument from which the music flowed, in front of people, was something that was way too scary. And so I kept this music only to myself and away from the ears of any other people in the world.

Then one year at a conference for the Voices In Action Organization, where I felt safe, I decided to share it in the talent show. I was scared to death as my time came for me to perform on the piano, and even though I thought about backing out, I knew that it was time to take this step and share my music with others. As I approached the piano, my feet were shaking and hands trembling, but I continued to tell myself to relax and ignore the fact there were many other people in the room. I kept telling myself that I was just going to have fun and let the music flow out of me. My plan was to place my hands on the piano, and wherever they rested, I would begin playing. What happened next not only mesmerized the people in the room, but what came out shocked me. I knew that it was truly the music, the language, from a deep place within me.

For years to follow, the music lay dormant, and for a long time it was a connection to a source of pain in my life. In those moments when I endured some difficult times at the hands of monsters in my life, this music would transcend me into another realm of the world. It was my safe place. It was my language that I could scream and cry through, which no one else understood. The notes were words that could not be spoken and tears that could not be shed. So for me to begin connecting myself with the music, I had to deal with the pain it brought forth -- for that which carried me through life for many years also allowed me to shut out so much of what I had to feel.

As time went by, I began to heal from these traumas of the past, and the music began to grow and become alive within me. The notes once again sang out their melodies, and they connected as a language of survival and connection to better things yet to come. This time, the songs that I once knew by memory were no longer of use, for all my hands wanted to do was to create what was coming from deep within. Finally, I gave in and began allowing myself to be connected to the music, and from that point forward, I created some very beautiful music.

At first all I was able to do was to record the music by way of a tape recorder. Once I did this, I was shocked at what I heard. What my ears heard was much different than what I thought was actually created. It was the first time that I actually heard what was being played. Even though I managed to put the notes together, I never actually heard what was being played until it was played back. While that may sound strange, it is true. Using the computer to hear the music for the first time has been so enlightening and so healing as well.

This has been my journey and for the first time in my life, I am sharing this with the world. It is a great joy to see how the language of the notes affects those that listen to the music. Unfortunately my mom left this world before this took place, so she never got to hear my finished music while she was on this earth. I do think, though, she has heard the music, because it was created from her in so many ways and from the emotions I experienced as a result of having to say goodbye to her.

Hopefully you will see that I have created something beautiful which came out of struggles from my past. It was a long road from which I am healing, and the healing still continues. My music also signifies that there are possibilities out there, which we may not even know about today, but may be introduced to in the future. Where the music will take me, I do not know. I just know that I will no longer hide it, but will trust myself to share this music with the world.

If you would like to listen to this music, it can be found on my website at www.donshetterly.com. It is a language that is not spoken but is connected by each note and each sound. I do hope that you can take a moment to listen to it, so you will be introduced to music that comes from the soul of a survivor. *(Written on 12/27/02)*

Tribute To My Mom

My mom was a very warm, compassionate, caring, and insightful lady. She was a beautiful lady that never showed her true age (much like myself and her father). She was more creative than I realized through cooking, baking cakes, and in just about everything she did. She was so intelligent, and saw things that most others in this world just don't see. She picked up on things that were going on with me, yet I never spoke about. She'd know what I was thinking and feeling right down to the detail, without me saying a word. She just seemed to know things, and to know how to navigate through life. I've only seen one other person who shows similar signs of just knowing things (and I don't mean in a general way but in a very detailed way), with an accuracy that is beyond my comprehension.

As I mentioned, she always wanted to take piano lessons, but because her alcoholic father spent their money on his beer with his Masonic Lodge friends, she never got to do that. Yet, she could sit down at my piano and pick out little tunes without knowing where a note was on the piano. Once I began to teach her some of the notes on the piano. She was the one responsible for making sure I had the opportunity to take piano lessons when I showed the desire for it.

She was the peacemaker in the family, much like I tended to be later on, until it took its physical toll on me. She worked for many years as a nurse in health care, especially trying to help the elderly. I worked in a nursing home when I was in high school doing maintenance, and loved every moment around the elderly, and now I also work in a health care related way.

She was a good communicator, both in speaking and in writing, although she considered herself to be shy, and I think she struggled with self confidence. She would often teach Sunday school classes that I was in, and she would often volunteer to put together Christmas programs for church. She answered the main phone, and was a receptionist for a long time in a couple of companies. Her voice was always so pleasant. She could be horribly sick that day, but you would never hear it on the phone through her voice. She tended to hide a lot from almost everyone.

Even in the midst of all that she endured (and we endured), she tried to show us compassion and love and understanding. She had her faults and her own mindsets, but she was more accepting and understanding in the world than most people. She was a very simple lady, not asking for or desiring much for herself. She, however, tried to do as much as she could for her family, and especially her children, with the limited resources she had. She tried to help me excel in every way that I could, and she tried to protect me as much as she could.

My mom was a very strong lady, through her personality and through what she would do physically. Yet if you saw her or were around her, she would seem very meek, mild, and like one of those people who you just enjoy being around. She made friends easily at church, and if someone needed something, she found a way to help out.

I remember having so many Sundays where our resources were limited, but she'd invite people over for our Sunday meal. She seemed to enjoy that. As a child, I remember her bringing some of the residents from the nursing home where she worked, home for Thanksgiving and Christmas, so they wouldn't have to spend it alone. Most of the time, these people played the piano, so it was an extra treat for me. And when we took them back to the nursing home, we would drive around town looking at the Christmas light displays.

I'm sure I'm missing half of the stuff about her, but she gave so much and if anyone showed me that love did exist in the middle of the horror I lived in, it was my mom. When my mom died, I had not been able to talk to her for the last 10 years and that made it difficult. However, I've seen very clear signs that she is around me constantly and supporting me.

There was a park in Miami that I went to shortly after I found out my mom had died in a car accident. It was one of my favorite parks. That day it was raining, but I saw the park bench where I was at have a gleam of sunlight shine upon it and the rain stopped in that specific moment while the rain continued around it.

Another year, I was there walking in the park with Jeff on the anniversary of her death, and it was a very hot and still day. The wind was not blowing at all until I was talking about her, and then it came up very strongly -- just in the exact place we were, at but in no other area of the park. I could tell, because I checked the trees for movement. I do feel her around me, and have had several people say they see her around me as well. *(Written on 5/10/04)*

Breathe

By Don Shetterly

Breathe in the good,

Breathe out that which you don't need.

Breathe in the energy, the strength, the sustenance for your life.

Breathe out that which holds you, constricts you, and binds you.

Breathe.

Breathe.

Breathe.

Life has so much to offer, not so little.

Life is about so much more, not what it doesn't have.

Life is about possibility, hope, and what can be.

Life is you, us, we, them, and everyone in between.

Life is all of us together connected so intricately.

Breathe.

Breathe.

Take it all in,

And know that all is, just as it is for this moment.

(Written on 6/14/09)

Chapter Thirteen

Closing Thoughts

We are a result of the journey we have walked. Each day that we have gives us the possibility of so much more. May we embrace all of it fully!

Selected Writings

Closing Thoughts

Closing Thoughts

I am amazed at just how far my own journey has taken me. Never did I realize many years ago just what was possible. It would have been difficult to convince me, in those dark moments, that healing of any type was possible.

For in my life, all I had seen were the depths of despair and I knew no other way. All seemed so dark in my life that even attempting to have hope was beyond comprehension. My mind did not know what hope and possibility meant, nor did I have the slightest clue how to grasp on to it. Often, my life felt out of my control and far from reality.

It was amazing that various people, events and circumstances crossed my paths at the exact right moment for me. For in those times, I did not know what to look for -- and if I thought I did, I would have been fooling myself. It was in these moments, where out of frustration and pain, I allowed myself to notice all that was there for me. Even at the time, I most likely didn't recognize all the support and assistance I had, but now as I look back I can see it much more clearly.

It is interesting that often when we are in the midst of difficult circumstances, that nothing seems to be connected and there doesn't appear to be a way out. It is only when we keep our feet moving forward on the poorly defined path that we find our way to the other side. Once to the other side, we began to get a glimpse of what we just passed through.

Many years ago when I was a child, I knew that there would be a difficult time I would pass through in my life. I knew many of the overall details that did emerge over the course of my life. Even knowing these things, I was still not prepared for all I endured. I was not ready for the difficult journey that awaited me. A journey is something one must travel through in order to experience. Without the travel, there is no way you would fully know what the experience was about.

I often see many people in the world that are hurting and have lost hope. They do not think there is any hope for them and it appears that if possibility is nothing but a dream. Giving up on life seems all too easy, while continuing to fight through another day seems nothing short of scaling up a mountain.

Who can blame these people though? Many have experienced much pain and frustration in their lives. They have seen very little that shows them there is anything better out there for their lives. They struggle each day not to live, but just to exist. It is difficult, and many have lost any hope they had. All they want is to be delivered from the daily reminder of all the pain they experience.

My heart weeps for each one of these people, for I was there in the midst of these moments as well. I remember the days that I could barely keep myself going, let alone exist or live in life. There were moments that I tried hard to give up and take my own life. There were moments that I hated everyone and anyone around me including myself. I fought to understand and comprehend all that I had gone through in life. I fought to have enough hope just to make it one more moment.

Somehow, I kept myself going, step by step. I found a drop of courage at the moments I so badly needed it. People crossed my life not a moment too soon to help lift me up from the quicksand I was sinking into. It happened all without me knowing it at the time. Yes, the paralysis was difficult to endure and pass through, but it gave me the much needed determination to keep going on in life. When I got so very tired of taking another step in healing and when I didn't think I could do anymore, I would look back to the days where I could not function physically. Coming back from paralysis taught me so much about healing, and it helped give me the courage, strength and sustenance to go further. Without it, I might not have made it through my journey.

There is so much about my life and journey that the world has not heard. It will be coming soon. Not that I wish to bore everyone with the difficult moments and details, but that I want to give hope to those that are walking in the evil they have faced. I know that my story needs to be told and that through my own healing, others are inspired and encouraged. I wish for my life to make a difference in the lives of others because without that, my journey through the evil and pain would be for very little.

I hope that as you have read these various writings, you have gotten a picture of hope and possibility in your mind. I hope that you can tell that even through traumatic events such as I've been through, there is hope and possibility. The story does not need to end by being taken under as a result of the trauma. There is healing. There is hope. There is possibility.

I'm not going to write that it is all easy to heal from, for if you are in the midst of despair, you know the true reality. What I will write is that there is a way through these things. No matter how dark and difficult life may look, there are brighter days ahead, if we allow them to come into view. It is all up to us. Others may come along and help hold our hands through the roughest of moments, but in the end, our healing is possible by jumping off into the unknown. It is through embracing fear that we will find our freedom. It is a growing process that gives a little more to us each day that we are alive.

No matter what you may be experiencing in life, celebrate all that there is and all that you have. Use the examples I have shared in this book to help you understand that hope and possibility do exist. There is so much more out there than we often can see in this moment. If we allow ourselves to find that awareness, then we have truly evolved and become more human.

Chapter Fourteen

Resources

There are many that walk among us.
They may not always be visible but
they are surely walking beside us and
offering their support.

<u>Selected Writings</u>

Resources

Resources

Many of these links and acknowledgements were used throughout this book as reference. Each resource holds a special place in my heart and has been very helpful to me in my own healing process. Please visit my website www.donshetterly.com, for more information or for updates

1) **Dr. Paul Canali, Evolutionary Healing Institute**
   7800 Red Road, Suite 325, Miami, FL, 33143.
   Phone: 305-667-8174
   Website: http://evolutionaryhealinginstitute.com/

2) **Emma Wallace, RN, MS**
   Licensed Marriage and Family Therapist
   Website: http://www.sundancemft.com

3) **Educating Hands School Of Massage**
   Miami, FL. 305-285-6991
   Website: http://educatinghands.com

4) **Official Website Of Don Shetterly**
   Healing Piano Music, Books, Blog & Workshops
   Website: http://www.donshetterly.com

5) **Mind Body Thoughts Blog**
   A blog dedicated to healing and development in the area of how our minds and our thoughts connect with our awareness.
   Website: http://mindbodythoughts.blogspot.com/

6) **Trish Kalhagen, Sacred Moments**
   Reiki, Spiritual Direction, Labyrinth Workshops
   Edgerton, WI. 53534, 608-921-1123
   Email: sacredsharing@yahoo.com

7) **CD:** *Songs For The Inner Child* by Shaina Noll
http://www.shainanoll.com/

8) **The Trager Approach®**
http://trager-us.org/
The Trager® Approach is a pleasurable, gentle and effective approach to movement education and mind/body integration; the effects are deep and long-lasting.

9) **The Male Survivor Organization**
Overcoming sexual victimization of boys and men.
Website: http://www.malesurvivor.org/

10) *On Becoming An Artist, Reinventing Yourself Through Mindful Creativity* by Ellen J. Langer
Ballantine Books, ISBN: 978-0-345-45630-4

11) *The Invitation* by **Oriah Mountain Dreamer**
Harper San Francisco Books,
ISBN: 0-06-251-584-5

12) **Song:** *Angels Of Comfort* by Iasos
http://iasos.com

13) **Official Website of Yanni**
http://www.yanni.com/

14) *Hidden Messages Of Water*
by Dr. Masaru Emoto
Beyond Words Publishing, ISBN: 1-58270-114-8

15) *The Mind Body Prescription: Healing The Body, Healing The Pain* by **Dr. John E. Sarno**
Warner Books, ISBN: 978-0446675154

16) MD Andersen Cancer Center, Orlando, Florida
Labyrinth. Address: 1400 South Orange Ave,
Orlando, FL. 32806
Website: http://www.orlandohealth.com

17) Touch Research Institute
http://www6.miami.edu/touch-research
Miami, FL.

Chapter Fifteen

Discussion Guide

We all start from a tiny fragment of substance, and find ourselves created into a work that is ever changing and evolving.

Selected Writings

The following pages give a framework for a 12 week, group discussion guide or even a study guide for personal use. My hope is that you will find others who could benefit from reading this book and form a group to discuss and learn from it. While I have included questions for discussion, feel free to be creative in how you approach this book. The discussion guide is just a framework. If you form a group, please feel free to email me and let me know how it impacted your lives.

Group Discussion – Chapter One
Introduction and My Story
(Week 1)

Suggested Exercise:
Write your own story, and include many details in it. See if you can write it from a standpoint that gives hope and possibility. Make sure it captures all the emotion and feelings that you can connect with.

Discussion Questions:
1) Do you believe we all have hope and possibility for our lives?

2) Do you believe there is hope and possibility for **YOUR** own life?

3) After reading "My Story" on page 6, what parts are difficult to read?

4) After reading "My Story" on page 6, what do you see as good coming from a story like this?

5) How much are the experiences you have faced in your life locked up within your own body? Give an example.

6) What does it mean to you that we are all meant to be much more than we currently are?

Closing Thought:
Out of difficulty, wonder can emerge.

Group Discussion – Chapter Two
Hope Of Possibility
(Week 2)

Suggested Exercise:
Try exercise on page 29, *Concern And Worry*

Discussion Questions:
1) What is something in your own life that you feel is impossible for you to do or face?

2) How could you reframe the impossible from question #1, in your mind?

3) What situation have you experienced in your life that you doubted you could make it through but you did?

4) How did you make it through this experience from question #3?

5) If there is an impossible situation you are currently experiencing, what one step could you take at this moment to begin moving forward?

6) Describe how your life is like a storybook.

Closing Thought:
We've seen ordinary people do extraordinary things and accomplish tasks that were nothing short of impossible at the time.

Group Discussion – Chapter Three
Self Acceptance
(Week 3)

Suggested Exercise:
#1: Write out your own poem or thoughts of self acceptance. (See page 38)

#2: Consider creating a Navigation Of Life Chart (See pages 40-43)

Discussion Questions:
1) What limitations do you put upon yourself?

2) How have you navigated through difficult moments in life?

3) What items would you offer at a garage sale for your life?

4) Name one big struggle you face in life, and ask yourself are you ready to let go of it?

5) Do you believe you can let go of it (answer to #4)? Why or why not?

6) If you opened the closet door of your life, what might you find inside?

Closing Thought:
I completely love and accept myself.

Group Discussion – Chapter Four
Rewiring The Brain
(Week 4)

Suggested Exercise:
Write out an affirmation for your current life. (See page 78)

Discussion Questions:
1) Can you identify signs in your body that you are numbing yourself to some experience from your life?

2) How do you notice fears in your day from sources around you?

3) What are your top five fears?

4) How is fear a good thing to your life? Example?

5) How has your sense of what is real or unreal changed for you in your life?

6) What clouds from your own life are you thankful for?

Closing Thought:
To rewire our brain, is to give us new paths to explore.

Group Discussion – Chapter Five
Personal Growth
(Week 5)

Suggested Exercise:

1) #1: Make a list of things in your life that you want to let go of. You could either burn the list as a symbolic gesture of letting them go, or place a pebble for each item in a jar of water to represent the water washing them away.

#2: Take the Self Test at www.hsperson.com for highly sensitive people.

Discussion Questions:

1) Record your observations to the exercise on page 99.

2) In what ways do you ignore your own body pain? Example?

3) What fears hold you back for discovering your true self?

4) Identify one way that you are critical or judgmental.

5) Take an inventory of how you spend your time. Do you like the results?

6) How would you change the way you spend your time in life?

Closing Thought:

To grow and evolve as humans is one of the greatest gifts we can give ourselves. To grow and evolve is to be human.

Group Discussion – Chapter Six
Our Body Connections
(Week 6)

Suggested Exercise:
Sit quietly with yourself and observe your breath. How deep or shallow is it? What is the rhythm of it? What do you notice about it? How does it make you feel? Is this a safe experience or not? Record your thoughts.

Discussion Questions:
1) What do you think of when you hear the word massage? Bodywork? Healing?

2) How often do you receive some form of bodywork and why?

3) What positive results do you see in massage?

4) Do you think it is easy for you to relax? Why or why not?

5) What holds you back from connecting with your body?

6) How often do you check in with your breathing in a day?

Closing Thought:
Let us be mindful and connected to our bodies.

Group Discussion – Chapter Seven
In The Moment
(Week 7)

Suggested Exercise:
Search your local area for a labyrinth and walk it. Draw from its energy and from your own pausing to gain new insights for your life. Record your thoughts.

Discussion Questions:
1) What does being mindful mean to you?

2) What does it mean to be the observer in your life?

3) What is your reaction when you make a mistake?

4) How would you change your reaction to a mistake that you make?

5) Pause for a moment and allow yourself to look at a difficult situation. Explain what you see or feel when you do this.

6) If you were going to be walking the labyrinth, is there a question you are waiting to be answered at this time?

Closing Thought:
The greatest moment we have in our lives is the moment we are experiencing. Anything past is already gone, and the future has not yet arrived.

Group Discussion – Chapter Eight
Connections
(Week 8)

Suggested Exercise:
Say something nice to people you meet today, or offer them a smile and observe their reaction you get. Record your observations and your own reactions.

Discussion Questions:
1) List several people you know and then list a word or phrase next to their name that says something nice about them.

2) When you have gone through difficult times, what have been the most helpful things others have done for you?

3) What are some ways you can show others you care when they are going through difficult times?

4) Take a moment and just pause. Notice and focus on your breath for 30 seconds. Then take a moment and connect with your heart by feeling the love you have for various people in your life. Record your observations.

5) After you have finished question #4, how do you feel?

6) After question #4, what changes (if any) do you notice in your body?

Closing Thought:
A smile or a cheerful hello is worth more than all the gold in the world.

Group Discussion – Chapter Nine
Music Connects Us
(Week 9)

Suggested Exercise:
Pick out a song that you enjoy and see how many dimensions of it you can hear (See page 157). Consider sharing this exercise with others.

Discussion Questions:

1) From the suggested exercise, can you identify how these different dimensions affect you emotionally?

2) Again, from the suggested exercise, how do you notice or feel the different dimensions of the music in your body?

3) What does the music you listen to say about your life?

4) What one song could you play right now that would offer encouragement to your day?

5) Have you ever made a "power" CD where you picked your all time favorite encouraging songs, which you played before major moments in your life? What songs would be on your CD?

6) Consider playing beautiful and relaxing music during your day to help keep your mind focused and relaxed. Observe what happens when you do this and journal your thoughts.

Closing Thought:
Music touches our souls, enlightens our minds and carries us forward.

Group Discussion – Chapter Ten
Listening
(Week 10)

Suggested Exercise:
Quiet your mind, play some peaceful music, or sit outside in nature for this exercise. Close your eyes, focus on your breath, and relax your mind. Allow yourself to just write, scribble, draw, whatever comes out of your hands.

Discussion Questions:
1) During the suggested exercise, what did you notice or create?

2) In what ways does this exercise show you just how much information you hold within yourself?

3) What experiences in life have helped you become more aware that the answers we seek are within us? Example?

4) What are some reasons we miss things in our day?

5) Are there situations that have taken place in your life that show you angels or some other forces are at work? Explain.

6) In what ways are we mindless in our day? Examples?

Closing Thought:
If we listen with our hearts, our minds and our bodies, then we will truly hear that which is meant for us.

Group Discussion – Chapter Eleven
Abundance
(Week 11)

Suggested Exercise:
Create a gratitude jar (See page 174)

Discussion Questions:
1) List the good things in your life at this moment.

2) Take a moment to think about something you want to achieve. Picture in your mind all the steps you would do to accomplish this, and record your observations.

3) What reality are you creating at this very moment?

4) What reality would you like to be creating in your day?

5) How do you allow or not allow good things in your life?

6) What one thing could you identify and change today that would change your focus and allow abundance in your life?

Closing Thought:
Let us be thankful for all we have, for we are truly blessed.

Group Discussion – Chapter Twelve
Special Moments & Closing Thoughts
(Week 12)

Suggested Exercise:
Write your own story about a special moment in your life.
Share it with others.

Discussion Questions:
1) What story from this chapter has impacted you most?

2) How do our moments in life come together to impact others?

3) If someone was going to write about a moment where you impacted their life, what moment would that be?

4) How can you share your life and talents with others?

5) In what ways has this book changed your life?

6) What were your favorite parts of this book?

Closing Thought:
We are a result of the journey we have walked. Each day we have gives us the possibility of so much more. May we embrace all of it fully!

Index

About The Author

Don Shetterly is a licensed massage therapist specializing in trauma release and healing the mind body connection. In addition, Don is an accomplished pianist who creates beautiful, heart-felt and relaxing piano music. Don is also the creator of the Mind Body Thoughts blog. In his spare time, Don enjoys painting, writing, and all the wonderful moments in life.

About Don's Music

Make sure you check out Don Shetterly's relaxing piano music on his website at www.donshetterly.com . Don began releasing relaxing piano music in 2003, and has put out several singles along with full length CD's *Dancing With Life*, *Focusing*, *Relaxing Spa Music*, and *Christmas Songs*. You can find all of Don's music on iTunes, Amazon and many other online digital stores around the internet.

Donation

The author is donating 10% of the profits from this book to the Male Survivor Organization. Male Survivor is an organization committed to preventing, healing and eliminating all forms of sexual victimization of boys and men through support, treatment, research, education, advocacy and activism. Visit www.malesurvivor.org for more information.

Made in the USA
Monee, IL
20 May 2021

69152268R00134